LANCASHIRE EVENING
Telegraph

IMAGES OF

East Lancashire

LANCASHIRE EVENING

Telegraph

IMAGES OF

East
Lancashire

ERIC LEAVER

The Breedon Books
Publishing Company
Derby

First published in Great Britain by
The Breedon Books Publishing Company Limited
44 Friar Gate, Derby, DE1 1DA
1993

ISBN 1 873626 63 0

Printed and bound by Hillman's Printers, Frome, Somerset.
Jacket printed by BDC Printing Services Limited of Derby.

Contents

Images of East Lancashire . . An Introduction

IT IS fortunate for us that photography developed from being an art, science and pastime for only a very few into a popular hobby and not-so-unusual occupation just at the time that it did.

For, what the free-roving camera lens saw was a dynamism unparalleled in East Lancashire's history — the age when our region was at the climax of its remarkable growth from virtual unimportance to a position of tremendous economic importance, not just nationally, but globally.

The Industrial Revolution had its very origins in East Lancashire. Cotton, coal and metal were the materials of a formula that produced this tremendous change. Villages became towns as people rushed in. More and more mill chimneys raked the skyline. Houses, schools, churches sprang up and spread ever further.

But the story of this immense social and economic phenomenon is well-known and well-documented. And it is not the purpose of *Images of East Lancashire* to go over this familiar saga, but, rather, to look at what it produced.

Here is the era when town halls, market places, fire-engines and tramways were still new — and symbols of the new wealth and civic pride that went into the making of corporations and public institutions.

Here we see the age when the social sub-structure created its own building boom — of steeples, orphanages, teetotal missions, giant music-halls and theatres and public houses galore.

And all of it had a character and individuality now so missing from the more bland townscapes that have replaced them.

It may be, then, with a sense of ruefulness that we look at what we have lost. But so, too, it must be remembered have many of the demerits of that exciting era disappeared — the workhouse, child labour, the fever hospital, the soot and so many of the slums.

The main purpose of this book, however, is not to lecture on the role that preservation and conservation ought to have had in the shaping of our townscapes and communities as we see them now. Rather, the intention of *Images of East Lancashire* is to entertain, to create interest and curiosity, and to spark the reader's nostalgia and recollections.

With this in mind, efforts have been made to show as much as possible of what has changed in East Lancashire. The book has no fixed theme — other than to progress from images of the region's larger towns to those of its smaller ones and of its villages before taking a detailed look at the social life that existed there.

There are also sections on East Lancashire at work and on the region's transport of the past. We also take a glimpse at wartime and at the worst the weather could do.

With the exception of the colour photographs on the dust jacket — kindly lent by the Publicity Department of Blackburn Borough Council — all the pictures in this book have come from the archives of the *Lancashire Evening Telegraph*. A great many have been taken by the newspaper's own photographers, but many have also been given down the years by the public libraries and museums in Lancashire, by private collectors and by readers, all of whom we gratefully acknowledge as the original sources.

The publishers also wish to thank the staff of the editorial library of the *Lancashire Evening Telegraph* for their assistance in the creation of *Images of East Lancashire.*

Blackburn

Market Place, Blackburn, 1900, with Victoria Street in the background. Twice a week — Wednesdays and Saturdays — the sett-paved square and its vicinity became a canvas-covered bazaar of market traders' stalls — with more than 350 of them supporting Blackburn's boast of having the finest open retail market in the country. The spot was also home to the town's Easter fair and, on Sundays, it attracted open-air preachers, political orators and buskers. The market moved to its present indoor site at the end of 1964 — after which the square and these fine buildings disappeared to make way for the town's new shopping precinct. Note the hot potato vendor's cart, far right.

Church Street, Blackburn, *c*.1913. Most of the buildings in this view have disappeared. Beaty Brothers' outfitter's store on the corner of Victoria Street (right) stands on the present-day site of Yates' Wine Lodge. Across the road, where the Army, Navy and Air Force careers office now is, Saxone and Cable Shoes.

Salford, Blackburn, under water on 12 November 1901 — the day a 16-hour downpour turned the River Blakewater, normally a trickle, into a torrent that spilled over town-centre Salford Bridge. Here, looking from Church Street, past the ivy-clad home of Rural District medical officer Dr William Pollard on the corner (left), down Holme Street to the aptly-named New Water Street (right), we glimpse the frontage of the Theatre Royal in Ainsworth Street beyond. Inside, the flood reached the height of the stage. People whose homes and shops were flooded blamed the Corporation which had built a dam downstream near the town's electricity works. It cost the council £3,500 in compensation. Note the beer barrel washed up against the tramways cable post, far right.

Salford Bridge, Blackburn, 1898-1901. The date of this view is narrowed down to this period as it was in 1898 that the Corporation in whose livery the tramcar (left) is painted, bought the town's tramways from the syndicate which started services in 1885 with a mixture of horse and steam traction. The lack of overhead wires indicates that the tramcar belongs to the steam era which did not end on the Salford Bridge-Cemetery route until July 1901. Here, a pair of horse-drawn omnibuses compete for passengers. The ornate combined drinking fountain and lamp standard in the middle of the picture was removed in the 1920s and its remains are now in Pleasington Playing Fields, Blackburn.

Preston New Road, Blackburn, around the turn of the century. In the background is St George's Presbyterian Church which opened in 1868 and was demolished soon after its closure in 1974.

Salford, Blackburn, from Holme Street about 1910. Beneath the tramlines and the expanse of granite setts covering Salford Bridge flows the River Blakewater, turned into an underground stream at this spot some 25 years previously. The gabled buildings in the background still stand. To the right of Thomas Cook & Son's Tourist, Excursion and Shipping Office, with its awning lowered against the sun, stands the confectionery business begun by Alderman James Boyle, who came to the town in 1818, aged 14, and after an apprenticeship with a barber-cum-toffee maker made a reputation with his own sweets and earned himself the nickname 'Toffee Jem'. The Jap Nuggets advertised on the shop front were differently-coloured cubes with a coconut filling. The business closed between the wars.

Contrast the 'modern' 1910 view of Salford Bridge (above) with E.Vernon's painting of the spot prior to the 1840s.

Seen from another angle, Salford in 1899. The White Bull Hotel (left) on the corner of Church Street and Railway Road still stands, but is no longer residential. The building dates from 1852, but there has been an inn on the site for centuries.

The Theatre Royal, Ainsworth Street, Blackburn, in the 1880s. Built in 1816, it replaced the 'New Theatre' known to have stood on or near the site in 1787. To the left of the theatre was a beerhouse known as the Garrick's Head.

The new Theatre Royal, replacing the one shown on the opposite page (bottom), opened on 20 September 1886, with the play *My Sweetheart* and was described as a 'monument to the enterprise of Mr J.F.Elliston, the proprietor'. It was here in 1903 and 1905 that Charlie Chaplin did two stints as a teenage actor — in between playing billiards at his lodgings in the Haymarket pub around the corner in Cort Street.

In 1931, the Theatre Royal became a cinema. The building was pulled down in 1936 and replaced in 1937 with the purpose-built cinema that stood for 30 years before being consumed by Blackburn's dash for demolition and redevelopment.

Opposite Blackburn Town Hall in King William Street, the Exchange Hall still stands. Pictured here around 1909, it was opened in 1865 and served as the base of a weekly cotton market and, at other times, for meetings, entertainments and lectures. Charles Dickens, Lloyd George and Ramsay MacDonald are among the personalities who spoke there. Silent films were first shown at the hall in 1908, but it was converted into a cinema proper — the Majestic — in 1924 and is the Unit Four Cinema today. The building has another, looser connection with Dickens whose last public reading in the provinces was given there in 1869. In this picture, to the right of the entrance, is the office of whisky distillers William Grant & Sons — opened by the firm in 1904 as its first branch outside Scotland. It was founder William Grant's uncles, Manchester calico printers William and Daniel Grant, who were the inspiration for the characters, the Cheeryble brothers, in Dickens' novel *Nicholas Nickleby*.

Blackburn Town Hall, *c.*1900. Opened in 1856, five years after the town received its Charter of Incorporation, it cost some £35,000. Until 1912, when they transferred to the Sessions House in Northgate, the town's police offices were also accommodated here.

The Market Hall, Blackburn, stood a few strides down King William Street from the Town Hall. It was planned together with the Market Place and opened in 1848 while the smaller Fish Market extension (right) was added in 1870-72. The Market Hall's 72ft Italian-style tower was topped by an 18ft mast holding a copper ball, 4ft in diameter and 15st in weight, which provided Blackburn with a daily 'event'. Each weekday at noon, the ball rose up the pole and dropped an hour later — giving the signal for the firing of the town's One O'Clock Gun which was heard four days a week until 1931. Here, with the time on the tower's clock showing noon has passed and the ball at the bottom the pole, we get a clue to the date of the picture — some time after 1903 when the pole and ball went out of action until October 1924. The tower was toppled in December 1964, as Blackburn's central redevelopment drive began in earnest. Note the tar boiler at the centre of the picture. Chesty children were made to breathe the fumes from such boilers in the belief that it did them good.

The Market Hall clock tower coming down in 1964 after 116 years. The clock mechanism, dating from 1889, is in Liverpool's Museum.

Darwen Street, Blackburn, about 1920. The large building (centre right) was the town's Head Post Office from 1907 until 1972. In the distance beyond can be seen the chimneys of the Old Bull, the town's premier hotel.

Victoria Street, Blackburn, at its junction with Lord Street (left) and Ainsworth Street (right) about 1900. Here, facing the stalls on the Market Square, four grocery and tea stores compete with each other on the approach to the Liberal Party's Reform Club (centre right) which opened in 1866. These buildings were among the earlier casualties of Blackburn's 1960s redevelopment. The site is now completely covered by the town's main shopping precinct.

Fruit stalls on Blackburn Market, *c.*1906. These have their backs to the side of the Town Hall between King William Street and Tacketts Street. Clogs, cloth caps and starched collars also point to the period.

The full bustle of Blackburn's old open market is captured in its last year, 1964, in this view of the fruiterers' and butchers' stalls which fronted the Market Hall.

This shows the end of the old Blackburn market, with a stallholder on Market Street marking the occasion with a special sale.

Looking down Market Street towards Victoria Street in the 1930s. This section of the open market (left) was the location where bonneted ladies from Southport sold shrimps. On the corner with King William Street (right) stood Victoria Buildings which from 1902 to 1966 housed the well-known grocers E.H.Booth & Co and contained the first cafe opened by the firm.

Inside Blackburn's old Market Hall, September 1964.

The Market Hall tower, seen from the front of the Town Hall, about 1914. The Corporation abandoned efforts to grow trees outside the building, replacing them with four ornate lamp standards in 1934, after it was decided that 'severe cross winds' stopped them flourishing.

Church Street, Blackburn, about 1850. These long-gone buildings stood opposite the present-day site of the Yorkshire Bank. The picture was taken prior to widening of the street in 1874. Pickering's shop, with its distinctive crenellated frontage, sold brushes made on the premises. It was founded in 1825 by Peter Pickering who died not long before this picture was taken. His widow stands in the doorway of the shop. Next door (right), are the branch office of the *Preston Herald* newspaper and Sagar's grocer's shop — both tenants of Pickering's.

Looking up Church Street, Blackburn, from Salford about 1905. In the centre of the picture stand the railed entrances to the underground public conveniences which closed in 1962, ahead of the town-centre redevelopment which also removed Boot's chemist's and stationer's store from the spot it had recently occupied when this picture was taken. In the block at the left about this time — between Holme Street in the foreground and Victoria Street, where Beaty Bros clothiers' store is seen — were the climber-covered home of Dr W.R.Pollard, a clothing club, the town office of Appleby's millers, the Royal Commercial Hotel, Astley's stationers, Cowburn's umbrella manufacturers, Sellers' fishmonger's, the Golden Lion public house and Parker's boot dealers.

The Golden Lion Hotel, Church Street, Blackburn, in 1958 a few months prior to its closure in June that year. Once a noted coaching house, it continued its links with horse-drawn travel even after World War One— as the base for John Bull Tiger Services wagonette trips to Blackpool. According to folklore, a pillar in the pub's Tudor Room marked the centre of Blackburn.

Church Street, Blackburn, looking towards Salford just prior to World War One. In the background is the Bay Horse Hotel, one of the town's oldest coaching inns and figuring in its affairs in the 1790s as the starting point for journeys to Manchester. In 1826, it was commandeered by the Luddite mob in the power loom riots and was drunk dry. The building seen here was associated with the 1882 improvements of the Salford area which created the large open space where once stood the humped bridge over the now-underground River Blakewater. Both the former Bay Horse and the nearby Lord Nelson were demolished, set back some 50ft from their original sites and rebuilt. The last Bay Horse was demolished in 1963.

A closer view of the Bay Horse Hotel. The 1952 roadworks in the foreground are for the creation of a traffic roundabout. Beyond, at the junction of Salford and Penny Street is the Lord Nelson which closed in January 1963. On the building can be seen the OBJ — 'Oh Be Joyful' — sign advertising a brand of beer brewed at Dutton's nearby Salford brewery.

Looking across the expanse of Salford, Blackburn, in the 1930s towards the junction of Holme Street (right) and Church Street. The turreted building on the corner is the offices of Blackburn Corporation Tramways which moved to new premises in nearby Railway Road in 1938. The 'Belisha' beacons, warning drivers of pedestrian crossings, were a measure introduced in 1934. This tells us that the picture was taken in the intervening period. Around the corner, in Ainsworth Street, Turner's household furnishers is indicated by the firm's advertisement for Pioneer Cut Gear Mangles. Next door to the Tramways offices in Church Street is Woolworth's '3d and 6d Store'. The company quit Blackburn in 1986, 60 years after opening its original store in Church Street and extending the premises in 1938 and 1958 so that they occupied this view almost entirely. Further up the street is Astley's newsagents, a business that had been on the spot since the turn of the century.

Thwaites' Arcade, linking Church Street with Lord Street, Blackburn, was built on the site of some ancient tenements and is seen here from the Lord Street end. Above each entrance was a date stone for 1883, and the coat-of-arms of the man after whom it was named, Blackburn brewer and the town's one-time MP, Daniel Thwaites. Despite the date carved in stone, the arcade of 22 shops and two more flanking each entrance did not open until the following year. One of the coats-of-arms was restored to Thwaites' brewery's museum in 1987 — 16 years after the Arcade was demolished.

Victoria Street, Blackburn, c.1891 — on the short remaining section now known as Grosvenor Way. From the right, the picture shows Nos. 8 and 10 Victoria Street — the premises of hairdresser and tobacconist Thomas Kay and, next door, of oyster dealer Tom Molyneux whose other premises in King William Street are advertised on the shop front. The Stafford and Northampton Boot Manufacturing Company's shop is decked with footwear at the front and, at the side, with interesting advertisements, including some for men's headwear. The building with an entrance to the left of the hoardings is the vaults of the ancient Golden Lion Hotel whose front door was in Church Street.

Thwaites' Arcade, Blackburn, seen here illuminated with Christmas decorations in 1964, had a reputation for 'select' shops.

Looking up King William Street, Blackburn, in the 1950s. Prior to the 1830s, this spot was blocked off at Church Street by buildings — as it is today by the town's shopping precinct. The policeman on point duty stands on the spot of the ancient town cross which was erected in 1101, but which had entirely disappeared before 1840. Around the cross and from it, down Darwen Street, the old market spread. Monday was the market day, but from 1774 markets began to be held on Wednesdays and Saturdays instead.

An earlier view of King William Street, Blackburn, when the former Burton's tailor's store at its junction with the upper stretch of Church Street was the Prince of Wales Hotel. A policeman controlling traffic at this crossroads was a feature of the spot into the late 1960s.

The Boulevard, Blackburn, in 1922, with the statue of Queen Victoria in the background and, nearer, that of Gladstone. Behind the domed bulk of the Palace Theatre can be seen the chimney and wooden water cooling tower of the town's electricity works which opened on the site of the old gas works in Jubilee Street in 1895. The 250ft chimney was demolished in late 1925 and early 1926.

The Griffin area of Blackburn prior to World War One. The Griffin Inn, standing at the junction of Griffin Street and Redlam still dominates this spot, but the shops and the Redlam Inn in the row at the right have disappeared. In the 1890s, between the Griffin Inn and the main road's town-centre terminus at the top of King Street, less than a mile away, there were no fewer than 43 public houses — making up a daunting pub crawl that still lives on in legend. In the background of this view, a tramcar climbs Redlam brow, bound for Witton, while in the foreground, with a trolley, is a uniformed parcels delivery boy from the Corporation Tramways.

September, 1955. The Grand Old Man of British politics and of Blackburn's Boulevard since 1899, William Ewart Gladstone, is moved to a new home. The statue was relocated outside the Technical College building on Blakey Moor later that month, having been removed from the Boulevard because it was claimed it interfered with an improvement scheme. In 1983, the Liberal statesman's marble effigy was moved once more — to its present site at the junction of Northgate and New Market Street. The 12ft-high statue of the four times Victorian prime minister cost nearly £3,000 and was the first public memorial of him to be erected — despite Blackburn not having a strong Liberal tradition. A crowd of 30,000 witnessed its unveiling on the Boulevard by Gladstone's personal friend, the Earl of Aberdeen.

St John the Evangelist in Victoria Street, consecrated in 1789, is Blackburn's oldest church building and was the first chapel-of-ease to be built in the town. Its site and half its £8,000 cost were donated by eighteenth-century merchant prince, cotton magnate Henry Sudell. In 1800, it echoed to the sound of the first church organ in Blackburn. Closed as a church in 1975 and acquired by the town council, the Grade II listed building, with its Greco-Tuscan-style tower, stood empty for nearly 15 years before becoming a base for voluntary organisations. The inset shows the church's weather vane, depicting a reed and shuttle from a weaving loom — and commemorating master reedmaker Proctor Radcliffe's joining with the munificent manufacturer, Mr Sudell, in funding the tower's construction in 1802.

This horse trough stood outside the Griffin Inn for 60 years. It was donated in 1897 by the aptly-named Mr James Carter 'for the use of our dumb friends'. It also carried inscriptions saying: "A righteous man regardeth the life of his beast" and "He prayeth well who loveth both man, bird and beast." Removed at the same time in 1957 road safety measures were a police telephone kiosk and a public call box which occupied a spot alongside the horse trough.

Witton Stocks, Blackburn. Tram services first reached this spot in June 1889 — with horses doing the work. Almost ten years later, in March 1899, electric-driven trams, like this one on Redlam's descent towards Witton, arrived on the route. This tram, No.33, was one of the eight original open-topped Seimens types acquired by the Corporation. Shortly after World War One, they had glass screens and canopies fitted over the platforms. The absence of this on the tram in the picture suggests this view dates from some time in the first two decades of the century.

A few strides away from the tramway at Witton Stocks is this spot, pictured here some time between 1892 to 1909 — probably because of the grisly associations that the first of these years has with the scene. It was in November 1892 that nine-year-old farmer's daughter Alice Barnes was murdered here — where this bridge crossed the River Blakewater near present-day Buncer Lane. Young Alice was leading the cows from her family's farm at nearby Redlam to then-private Witton Park which stood behind the gateway (right) that disappeared with the linking of Buncer Lane to Preston Old Road. Alice died from suffocating on the handkerchief stuffed into her mouth by her assailant. Thrilled crowds flocked to the spot and a vigilante committee was set up at Witton as the police sought her killer. Eventually, they arrested sacked mill worker Cross Duckworth who had been drinking in nearby pubs on the morning of the crime. He was found guilty on purely circumstantial evidence and went to the gallows less than two months after Alice met her end. The tattered posters on the hoarding behind the bridge refer to swine fever precautions and an 1887 animal law about dogs. The boys each have iron hoops — a popular toy of the era.

Feniscliffe Brow, Blackburn. This spot on Preston Old Road, opposite the entrance to Witton Park — then the home of the Feildens who were the town's principal landowners and lords of the manor — is now far less rustic; the trees and grassy slopes to the left of the roadway having long been covered by factories and housing. The ornate stone cross across the road from the gateway to the park was erected by his mother as a memorial to Captain Randal Francis Feilden, of the Scots Guards, who died in 1886. It also incorporated a drinking fountain 'for the use of those Lancashire lads who, in life, he loved so well'. The cross was removed in 1930 with the widening of the road.

Beneath Preston Old Road, Blackburn, at Feniscliffe Bridge flows the River Darwen, meeting up inside Witton Park with the Blakewater on its way to the River Ribble. This view of the spot, looking downstream towards the bridge, dates from about 1914. Now, factory buildings flank the stream here. However, the rural character of the spot in this picture was flawed even then — by the heavy industrial pollution of the river.

Witton House, built in 1800, was the home of the Feildens, a major landowning and political family whose associations with Blackburn reach back to the sixteenth century. Replacing the earlier, much-older ancestral home which stood beside the Blakewater in Witton Park, this building was demolished in 1954 on falling victim to dry rot and decay after it and the surrounding 400-acre estate had been bought by the Town Council in 1947. Here, the neo-Georgian building and its owner, Lord of the Manor, Lieutenant-General Feilden, play host in 1888 to the Prince and Princess of Wales, later King Edward VII and Queen Alexandra, who had arrived earlier at nearby Cherry Tree railway station on their visit to Blackburn to lay the foundation stone of the town's Technical School. The royal couple, seen here in their carriage outside Witton House, took away with them a pair of clogs on an ebony stand — a gift from the children at Witton School. For the occasion, the Feilden family had the Latin salutation, 'Salve,' placed on the gable of their house.

Now a ruin, Feniscowles Hall, near Pleasington, on the outskirts of Blackburn, was built in 1808 by baronet Sir William Feilden, who was related to the Feildens, of Witton Park and lords of the manor of Blackburn. Surrounded by a deer park on the banks of the River Darwen, it occupied a pleasant spot — until pollution of the river became so bad that in the 1880s, this branch of the family decamped to the east coast, naming their new home at Scarborough 'Feniscowles House'. Afterwards, the hall and its gardens became a pleasure grounds — in which role, with ample benches for visitors, it is seen in this picture.

Outside the main gate to Feniscowles Hall prior to World War One. The sign advertises the pleasure ground's teas and refreshments as well as good accommodation and speedy catering for wedding and picnic parties.

The Old Bull Hotel, Blackburn, seen here in its hey-day as the town's premier hotel. This building dated from 1847, but the inn's antecedents stretched back at least 500 years and, in the era of stage coach travel, it was a major baiting point for the horse teams. It closed its doors in 1938, but was not demolished until 1950. Standing at the junction of Church Street and Darwen Street, it overshadowed the town's old Market Place. Above its 60 bedrooms, stood the hotel's kitchen — sited on the top floor to prevent cooking smells reaching the rooms below.

Inside the Old Bull's Spanish Room. The painting on the wall panels gave glimpses of Blackburn's past — one showing a handloom
weaver's cottage; the other, the Old Bull as it was 300 years earlier.

Several alternative cathedral designs were put forward in the 1930s by the architects charged with transforming Blackburn's former parish
church. This — envisaging a massive central lantern tower — was one which never became reality.

Blackburn Parish Church, 1910 — 16 years before it became a cathedral with the creation of the Diocese of Blackburn. Enlargement in keeping with its new status, began in the late 1930s — a process which, interrupted by the war years, was to take more than three decades to complete. This building was consecrated in 1826, six years after the demolition of the former parish church of St Mary the Virgin, which was built in the reign of Edward III, but whose origins reached back to Saxon times.

Seen, but not heard. In August 1948, the ten-strong peal of bells in Blackburn Cathedral's tower was removed for recasting, with extra weight being added to each one so that it would ring louder, in keeping with the cathedral status granted to the building in 1926. Six of the bells had been cast in 1737 — from metal of even earlier bells, it is believed — and originally hung in the tower of the old Parish Church. They were joined by the other four in its replacement in 1852. Shown here prior to its journey to the bell-founders, the peal returned beefed-up almost a year later.

Darwen Street, Blackburn, in 1929, with the soot-grimed Cathedral Tower glimpsed behind. All the property in the foreground was demolished in the 1970s. The two small shops at the left of the picture were once the humble house where Blackburn mayor and freeman, Alderman Henry Harrison was born in 1834. He rose to be one of Lancashire's cotton kings and, when he died in 1914, he left more than a third of his fortune to charity. At the right is the old Queen's Head Inn, on the street's corner with Dandy Walk. Named after Queen Anne, it was used by the military to hold prisoners in the 1842 riots in which striking Chartists attacked cotton mills, drawing the plugs from their boilers. Attempts by the stone-throwing mob to free the prisoners from a coach, resulted in the troops opening fire.

Darwen Street, Blackburn, in the late nineteenth century. The buildings in the centre of the picture vanished to make way for the town's new Head Post Office which opened in 1907. Behind the gas lamp at the left, stands the offices of corn merchants John and Henry Polding. Further down the street was a stationer's, a confectioner's, a tripe dealer's and a florist's. Next door, Ingram & Co, at the end of the block, manufactured bedding.

1854: Fish Lane, Blackburn, the line of which is now roughly covered by Cardwell Place. The house was the birthplace in 1750 of the first Sir Robert Peel, who became a wealthy cotton manufacturer and was father of the English statesman who founded the police service. He quit Blackburn for Staffordshire — later moving to Bury where his son, the future prime minister, was born — after rioting spinners, fearing the loss of their livelihoods to the new spinning jenny machines, attacked his factory premises in 1779.

The Palace Theatre, standing on the corner of the Boulevard and Jubilee Street, was Blackburn's Palace of Varieties. Opened in December 1899, on the site of livery stables and boasting the biggest gallery in Lancashire, it got off to an unfortunate start — with the company that ran it going into liquidation within six months. It re-opened in September, 1900, under the ownership of the McNaughton Vaudeville Circuit whose flagship theatre it became. Stars ranging from Harry Houdini to George Formby appeared there. Uncertainty, however, continued to dog the theatre — it was forced to close for four years in the 1930s and when it re-opened in 1936, it was as a cinema. Seen up for sale again in this 1950s picture, it spent its latter years as a dual-purpose cinema and bingo hall before closing its doors in October 1984, and being demolished in January 1989.

Penny Street, Blackburn, in the 1940s. Of this view, only the Fleece Inn (right), at the junction with Starkie Street, remains. The 2,000-seat Rialto Cinema, with its cafe capable of serving more than 150 people, was opened in December 1931, and was renamed the Odeon in 1957 before being demolished in 1974. The property across the road began to vanish in early 1963 as the first phase of Blackburn's central redevelopment aimed to find a new home for the town's market on the area between Penny Street and Ainsworth Street.

Looking up Penny Street, Blackburn, from town-centre Salford in the 1950s. Although this view has changed vastly, it helps us fix the locations of the following four photographs which were taken just prior to the 1882 improvements. These were to radically alter the area around Salford and the lower end of Penny Street — not least with the Bay Horse Hotel (left, behind the bus) and the Lord Nelson pub on the corner of Penny Street and Salford being moved back some 50 feet from their original sites to the locations seen here.

Here, we see the Lord Nelson's forerunner — the Bull's Head, or Roundabout, as it was popularly called, with the doorway to its vaults at the left of the cab parked off Salford. The cab could have belonged to the pub's landlord, Thomas Prescott, who, about the time this picture was taken, traded as a cab proprietor as well as a licensed victualler. The pub stood at the junction of Penny Street and Salford in Blackburn, just as its successor did after the corner was remodelled in 1882. But it was the next door beerhouse, named after England's sailor hero, — with the entrance in Penny Street — from which the 'new' Lord Nelson took its name. Higher up the street, by the gas lamp, is the shop of printer and paper dealer Joseph Sefton whose window posters give a clue to the date of the picture. They are advertising almanacs for 1882. This suggests that, when the camera captured this scene, that was the year or, possibly the one in view — with the big alterations it would bring to this part of the town centre. It may be, then, that the photographer was taking the opportunity to record the locality before it changed. Next door to Sefton's, the shop with the sloping ground-floor roof is that of furniture and hardware dealer John Jackson while beyond are the premises of grocer and tea dealer James Ainsworth.

Penny Street, Blackburn, c.1881-82. This is the stretch between Salford and Starkie Street. Saddler and harness maker Edward Haworth travelled from his home in Broomfield Terrace at Witton to run his business at No.8. His shop and the three-storey building to the right can be glimpsed behind the Lord Nelson pub in the 1950s picture of the area (previous page, bottom). Up the street to the right is the arched doorway of No.4 — the Lord Nelson Inn. Its landlord, Edward Cross, is also listed as occupying No.13 Salford around the corner, next door to the Bull's Head, suggesting that his pub straddled the rear of the other hostelry from Penny Street to Salford. The wares attracting the window shopper to the left of Haworth's shop are those of clothes dealer William Dyson.

In the centre of this picture is the shop of wholesale and retail tobacconist R.Worden — perhaps the man seen in the doorway in a white apron. He also doubled up as a hairdresser — a fact underlined by the barber's pole. His shop stood at No.5 Salford — in the middle of the separate short length of the street that lay between Penny Street and Salford Bridge in Blackburn. At the time this picture was taken, believed to be 1881-82, he also occupied other premises across the road at No.2 Salford. Next door, to the left, are the shuttered premises of provision dealer James Stanley who lived not far away in Mount Street, a spot now buried beneath the car park of Morrison's town-centre supermarket. Further down the street, also shuttered and covered with tattered posters, is a building not listed in the trade and street directory of the time. Do we, then, glimpse the 'old,' pre-1882 Bay Horse Hotel on Salford Bridge, awaiting demolition? Next door to Worden's shop at the right was the three-storey Mason's Arms whose landlady in 1881 was Mrs Agnes Carr. In the 1950s view of the spot, Worden's business can still be found on the short stretch of Salford between the Bay Horse at the left and Penny Street — to the right of which, under its protective sunblinds, is Weaver to Wearer men's tailors.

Penny Street, Blackburn, looking towards Salford — 1881-82. From the building jutting out at the left, these are the five premises, numbered 1 to 9, Penny Street. At the right, is the shop of chemists and druggists, Kenyon & Son, whose advertised wares include dog cakes, poultry meal, tobacco and Towle's Chlorodyne. Next door, plastered with newspaper posters, is Richard Arkwright's stationer's and newsagent's shop. To the left, the shop sign and the garment-hung frontage indicate that the premises are those of clothier W.Hirst — of which no mention can be found in Penny Street in directories of the period, although a shop of that name existed for many years in Victoria Buildings on the Market Place. However, above this perplexing name can just be glimpsed the name which restores sense and sequence to this scene's date and place. It is that of George Green who was listed there in 1881 as a clothier and pawnbroker — the latter being confirmed by the 'pop shop's' three brass balls over the door. Hirst, then, may have shared the premises or simply advertised his business there. In any case, the shop's other sign claims it was the 'oldest establishment for new and second-hand clothing' while the other panel said it had the largest stock of overcoats in Blackburn. Men's were priced at 15s; boys' at 5s 9d. Next door, to the left, was the shop of saddler John Irvin or Irwin and beyond is Miss E.Hacking's draper's. At the far left, we glimpse the three-storeyed Mason's Arms at No.7 Salford and, beyond that, the barber's pole of R.Worden (shown in the picture on the previous page) can just be seen sticking out. It seems fair to guess, then, that our old-time cameraman took this photograph from the same point in Penny Street from which he had captured, from a different angle, the picture of Haworth's harness maker's shop just across the street (page 42, bottom).

Salford, Blackburn, *c.*1910. The shop in the middle with the old-fashioned window is that of furniture dealer Harry Boyle who, at the time, also had premises in King Street. Next door, to the right, with a crowd of youngsters in front is Leeming and Yates saddlers' and to the left of the handcart on the pavement is the Ye Olde White Bull Hotel, which was established in 1750. It was pulled down at the end of 1959 to make way for a modern pub of the same name, but known since 1979 as the Brewer's Arms. The line-up outside Boyle's shop and the crowd being carefully kept on either side of it suggests the photographer was there for an 'occasion' — which may have been the forthcoming passing of the premises which were demolished afterwards, giving Calendar Street access to Salford.

Salford, Blackburn, *c.*1879. The original caption to this picture describes the buildings as 'Mr Thwaites' property' — an indication that they belonged to the estate of brewer Daniel Thwaites whose premises were nearby, off Eanam. In the background is the Starkie Street Foundry. Where the shops in this picture stood is now an open site, across the road from Morrison's town-centre supermarket. All except the Peel's Arms public house at the right disappeared soon after the picture was taken. The hostelry, whose landlady was Mrs Nancy Leach, served for many years as the premises of Rice's printers and was demolished only recently. About this time, the other businesses here were, from the right, a bird dealer's, a greengrocer's, a confectioner's and a furniture brokers.

Panoramic view of Blackburn from 'The Cannons' in Corporation Park. The spot from where this photograph was taken took its name from a pair of Russian cannons, captured at Sebastopol in the Crimean War, which the Secretary of State for War, Lord Panmure, presented to the town. The guns, both 24-pounders, arrived in Blackburn in June 1857, 12 months after the end of the war, and four months later, mounted on their specially-prepared site near the summit of Revidge, the guns roared again — at the celebrations marking the opening of the park. One of them was fired again in February 1914, by a protesting suffragette who exploded a home-made bomb inside the bore. Eventually, the cannons' wooden carriages rotted away and their muzzles sank into the gravel. Here, they are overshadowed by four German field guns, prizes of World War One. The German guns were sold for scrap in 1937 while the cannons disappeared in a World War Two salvage drive. The park's bandstand (far right) — and that of Queen's Park — went into the war effort's melting pot in 1941. The opening of the £2,000 bandstand, with a concert by the band of the Border Regiment in September 1909, drew a crowd of 6,000 to Corporation Park. The new bandstand, which replaced one built in 1880, was surrounded by seats for 2,300 people and was set in a large hollow which had been excavated by unemployed workers. This picture, showing the high ground in the distance covered by snow, was probably taken on a Sunday. During the week, the smoke from the forest of factory chimneys and thousands of domestic coal fires in the town beneath would have masked this view considerably.

The Fountain, Corporation Park, Blackburn, *c.*1908. The great fountain near the main entrance to the park was the gift of William Pilkington, Mayor of Blackburn at the time of the opening of the park in October, 1857. It was one of four fountains he donated. But the display provided by this one, with its 20ft spout, was not appreciated by all. On windy days, the water tended to blow on people sitting on the nearby benches and, in view of the £30 a year it would cost to make the fountain work satisfactorily, the Town Council voted in 1935 on making it into an ornamental flower bed by filling in its large lower basin. The site of the park itself — 50 acres and 18 perches — cost the town £3,257 when the Corporation bought it at £65 an acre from the Lord of the Manor, Joseph Feilden, in October 1855.

Sudell Cross, Blackburn, looking up Preston New Road, about 1900. This postcard picture is captioned 'Sunday Afternoon' and shows the now-abandoned custom of the promenade in full swing. Dressed in their Sunday best, folk went strolling up and down Preston New Road — the unattached younger ones being less concerned about the exercise and more about the prospect of 'clicking' with someone in the boy-meets-girl ritual, known colloquially as the 'Bunny Run' or 'Monkey Run'. In 1886, residents of Preston New Road were complaining about the nuisance caused by hundreds of young people gathering there and a police purge resulted in several teenagers being fined five shillings each for creating a disturbance. More shocking were reports that young respectably dressed girls in Preston New Road were making use of the 'most filthy language'. The photographer's shop in the background belonged to Edwin Hargreaves while next door were cycle dealers T.Walton & Sons.

Sudell Cross, Blackburn, looking down King William Street towards the Town Hall from Preston New Road, about 1900. This is one aspect of the town centre which has changed little in the interval. The tram tracks branching off to the right led to the tram shed in Simmons Street which housed the horse trams and horses used on the Preston New Road and Witton routes and also the steam trams from the Darwen route. The remains of the track can still be seen today where it enters the former shed.

New Market Buildings, on the corner of King William Street and New Market Street, Blackburn, 1908. Here, Worswick & Son sold furs, silks and mantles and illuminated their well-stocked windows with outdoor gas lamps. Around the corner, a trader's sign advertising boots and stirrups shows the horse age is still alive although the car parked nearby shows the motoring era had already begun in Blackburn. Today, Burton's menswear store occupies this spot and Worswick's first-floor showroom of 1908 now houses a fitness club.

The heart of Blackburn prior to redevelopment. This view of the area around old open market and the Market House with its clock tower was taken in September 1964, on the eve of the demolition and rebuilding orgy that gripped the town for 15 years. The extent of the transformation can be gauged from the fact that, of the buildings in this view, the only remaining ones are the Town Hall (right), the County Court building in Victoria Street (lower centre, facing the rear of the Town Hall) and some of the buildings in the block at the top right.

Peacock Row, Little Harwood, Blackburn. This vanished row of cottages, constructed of random stone, lay off Whalley Old Road, close to its present-day junction with Whitebirk Drive.

Blackburn Station and Boulevard. The electric tramcar near the centre of the picture and the steam-hauled ones at the left point to the photograph having been taken some time between 1899, when electric trams arrived in Blackburn, and 1901, when the steam variety disappeared. The station, little changed in its external appearance today, opened to passengers in September 1886, without any formal ceremony — probably because construction work was far from finished. However, the event was obviously regarded as an occasion by Mr S.Duckett, who issued the first ticket from the new office. Despite being the oldest employee and having lost a leg in the service of the railways, he stayed on duty all night in order to be able to do the honours the next day. The new building replaced the previous one which had served the town since the coming of the railway in 1846. The old station, about a quarter of the size of its replacement, with no booking hall and only two platforms just a few inches high, was built on land called Stonybutts somewhat further back than the new building and was largely hidden from view by a woodyard. The Lancashire and Yorkshire Railway paid £21,000 for the site of the new station and installed a clock in its turret that was guaranteed not to lose or gain five seconds in a month. Note the line of horse cabs waiting for custom. In the centre of the Boulevard stands the old cabbies' shelter which is said to have been part of an antique railway carriage.

The Boulevard, Blackburn, in 1927. Blackburn had no Corporation buses at this time. The white-topped buses in the distance and far right are in Ribble Motors' livery of the day and the other buses could be the Leyland 'G' types of the Blackburn Bus Company which ran services to Green Lane, Moorgate and Tockholes before being taken over by the Corporation in March 1931. Parked alongside the pavement are eight charabancs — perhaps indicating that this was a holiday period. The classic-style, white building at the right behind the row of London-style taxis is the cabbies' shelter. Costing £350 to build in 1913, it was the gift of a Mr William Ward, of Mellor. It was pulled down in 1944 because it 'impeded the flow of traffic'. In the centre background stands the building of the *Northern Daily Telegraph*, forerunner of today's *Lancashire Evening Telegraph*. It opened in 1894, eight years after the newspaper began publication. Its tower originally served as a loft for homing pigeons carrying reporters' despatches from football matches. The building was demolished in 1984 following the paper's move to new premises behind the row of buildings at the right two years earlier. The wide-open space of the Boulevard was created in improvement works carried out in 1884-85, associated with the building of the new railway station. Previously, the River Blakewater had flowed 'narrow, black and often noisome' along the edge of the churchyard at the left. The railed flower beds and fountain, glimpsed behind the row of charabancs, disappeared in improvements carried out in 1955.

A wintry scene on Blackburn Boulevard in the 1950s. The large, flat-roofed bus shelter was erected in 1937.

Railway Road, Blackburn, looking towards Salford Bridge, probably in the first decade of this century — called Station Road by the photographer. Next door to the *Northern Daily Telegraph* building at the right — separated by an alleyway that is now the approach to Morrison's supermarket — is the Temperance and Commercial Hotel with its ornate first-floor balcony. Next door, where the sunblinds shade the shop windows of piano and organ dealer James Eccles, is the double-fronted premises that were the *Telegraph's* first offices. Down on Salford Bridge, visible to the right of the covered cart in the centre of the picture, is the lamp-cum-drinking fountain that was moved in 1923 to Pleasington playing fields. Beyond, on the corner of Church Street, T.Walsh's tailor's shop occupies the then-newly-built turreted premises that were later to become the Corporation Tramways offices until 1937. By the chimney stack on the gable of the White Bull Hotel is a sign telling that John Haydock's livery stables were to be found up the archway at the left.

Railway Road, Blackburn, scene of a crisis in the early 1890s for the fledgling *Northern Daily Telegraph* which had set up business here at Nos. 19 and 21 in 1886. On the day this picture was taken, the gas engine which ran the newspaper's printing presses had broken down and it was found impossible to repair it in time for the day's first edition. All seemed lost until the paper's founder, T.P.Ritzema, had an idea. He called in the town's highways department and borrowed a steam-driven road roller. As the camera captures the scene, a curious crowd gathers to watch the drive belt run from the steam engine down into the newspaper's cellar and on to the machinery inside. Before long, the *Telegraph* — popularly known as "The Pink" after the colour of its pages in those days — was pouring from the press at the rate of 1,000 copies an hour. The day and the *Telegraph's* reputation of bringing out the news on time was saved!

Salford Bridge, Blackburn, 1958. Here, the River Blakewater disappears into the culvert created in the 1882 improvements to the area which included the removal of the old humped bridge and lowering road level by three feet. Six years after this picture was taken, the river and Water Street at the left were to disappear from view under the town's new market development. The bus stop was the town-centre terminus for the Wilpshire, Brownhill and Cemetery services.

The boating lake at Queen's Park, Blackburn. Originally known as Audley Recreation Ground, the park was named after Queen Victoria whose Golden Jubilee on 20 June 1887, was commemorated by the town with the official opening of the 33-acre park before a crowd of 20,000. Costing £15,000, the park took five years to create after the land was donated by the Ecclesiastical Commissioners with the proviso that the Corporation built a road around the site and an approach to it. The 3.65-acre lake was not completed until some years after the park opened. Its flotilla of rowing and sailing boats was immensely popular — so much so that, in 1936, the Corporation stopped leasing the boating rights to private operators and took over the business itself, adding motor-boats to the fleet, for which demand was so great that, on sunny days, would-be boaters had to queue for two hours.

Brownhill, Blackburn. Now the scene of a notorious traffic bottleneck where five roads intersect, this was still a sleepy spot on the town's outskirts when the cameraman captured this view. The overhead tram wires going along Whalley New Road towards Wilpshire were installed in 1902, but Brownhill Road (right), now filled with housing, is seen as a quiet country lane.

It was the arrival in the 1920s of the arterial road — creating a by-pass route to the north of Blackburn for traffic to and from Preston — that transformed Brownhill into a major junction. With the road scheme came large-scale housing development — the Corporation building more than 300 council houses at Brownhill and around newly-created Roe Lee Park nearby, some of which are seen lining the dual-carriageway Brownhill Drive at the right. The tram shelter at the bottom of Brownhill Drive also contained a telephone kiosk. St Gabriel's Church in the background (right) opened in 1933.

A forest of nearly 200 factory chimneys scraped Blackburn's skyline 50 years ago, testimony to the might of manufacturing over which King Cotton was predominant. But the biggest of the town's smokestacks was devoted to destruction, not production. Seen here with its 312ft of Accrington brick highlighted by the vestiges of a winter blizzard, the chimney of the Audley Destructor on the banks of the canal at Bennington Street cost the Corporation £2,550 to erect in 1888. Then, it was the tallest chimney shaft in the country. Its reign as a Blackburn landmark ended with its demolition in 1959 — a task which took the wrecking steeplejacks far longer than they expected, so sturdy was the old giant.

The Brownhill Arms public house and the row of cottages to the right are still a feature of this spot. This picture was taken in the mid-1920s when work had commenced on the building of Brownhill Drive in the foreground, part of the 4.25-mile arterial road scheme from Whitebirk to Yew Tree. Brownhill Cottages were originally much plainer, but each acquired bay windows in a 1914 renovation scheme.

The old Grammar School in Freckleton Street, Blackburn, looking across the graveyard of St Peter's Church. The single-storey school was built on Bull Meadow in 1825 and the ivy-covered master's house (right) was added in 1835. Originally, the school — established in 1567 by a royal charter by Queen Elizabeth I — was housed in the Lady Chapel on the south side of the old parish church and later in purpose-built premises erected in the churchyard. In 1882, the school moved from Freckleton Street to West Park Road, near Corporation Park. The classical pillar, seen left at the junction with St Peter's Street, was erected in 1853 by pupils as a memorial to Thomas Atkinson, headmaster for 20 years. It now stands at the school's present-day site.

The Old Toll Bar at Brookhouse, Blackburn. This building, which stood at the junction of Whalley New Road and Whalley Old Road, was one of several relics in the town of the turnpike era which petered out in East Lancashire in 1890. The toll house was demolished in 1928. In the distance (left) can be seen the steeple of now-vanished St Michael's C of E Church, which was demolished in 1986, six years after its closure and 117 years after its consecration.

The Grand Theatre in Jubilee Street was Blackburn's last 'live' theatre. Closed in 1956 — victim of the emerging TV age — it was demolished two years later. The first theatre on the site was a wooden building which burned down one Sunday night after a Salvation Army meeting was held there. It was replaced by the Amphitheatre which opened in 1880 and later became the Princes Theatre. It was rebuilt in 1906 as the New Princes before being called The Grand in 1928. Throughout its life, the theatre had to struggle against competition from the larger Palace and Royal theatres and later from no fewer than 14 cinemas in Blackburn. During that time, its fare varied from music-hall and repertory to local amateur shows and occasional 'Adults Only' performances. Among the stars who strode its stage were Dan Leno, Vesta Tilley, George Formby and Ted Ray. The site is now occupied by the town's telephone exchange.

Burnley

These Russian cannons mounted in the grounds of the old Burnley Grammar School at the junction of Colne Road and Bank Parade were trophies of the Crimean War. They were brought to the town in 1867 through the offices of General Sir James Yorke Scarlett, the hero of the Battle of Balaclava in October, 1854. The 55-year-old commander of the victorious Heavy Brigade had earlier made Burnley his adopted home after marrying Miss Charlotte Hargreaves, of Bank Hall, while he was stationed in the town. The guns were melted down for scrap in 1941 as part of the war effort. A 1988 plan to replace them with replicas, costing £10,000, was dropped by the Town Council.

The Culvert, Yorkshire Street, Burnley. Originally, the town-centre aqueduct carrying the Leeds-Liverpool Canal — which opened in Burnley in 1796 — had only the central archway. The smaller pedestrian 'gimlet holes' at the sides were added later. Here, preparatory work is under way on the 1926 new aqueduct scheme that considerably widened the roadway under the canal.

The Culvert, Yorkshire Street, Burnley — after the improvement works. This view dates from 1953.

Taken in 1936, this picture shows workmen removing the tram tracks at the junction of Gunsmith Lane and Yorkshire Street, Burnley — the lines having been made redundant with the town's abandonment of tramways the previous year. In the background is the old Keirby Brewery. At the left, part of the Yorkshire Hotel is glimpsed and centre right is Rishton Mill which was demolished for the building of the Odeon Cinema which opened in 1937.

The old Royal Oak Hotel in St James' Street, Burnley, pictured in 1896. The public house occupied this spot until making way for the development of the Marks and Spencer store at the street's junction with Curzon Street in 1935.

The Royal Hotel seen from another angle. Grimshaw's Sparkling Ales and Noted Stout, advertised on the pub's signs, came from the brewery which stood on the site of the present-day Keirby Hotel. Note the point-duty policeman's cape hanging on the Royal Oak's wall. The inset shows the same spot occupied by Marks and Spencer.

By 1953, when the Marks and Spencer store in St James' Street was decorated for the Coronation celebrations, the traffic-control policeman, who stood at the nearby junction with Curzon Street and Hammerton Street, had been replaced with automatic signals.

The Old Red Lion at the junction of St James' Street and Manchester Road was indeed old when this picture was taken. Outside its doors, until 1866, a weekly market was held — the spot being considered to be the centre of Burnley. The inset shows the spot occupied by the 'new' Old Red Lion, built in 1868-69.

Around the corner from the Old Red Lion, a stride or two up Manchester Road, is Red Lion Street. This is how it looked before 1922 when the Savoy Cinema was built on the corner then occupied by Holdsworth's butcher's shop. Here, a four-wheeled horse-drawn cab provides competition for a motor-driven taxi.

The Savoy Cinema, on the corner of Red Lion Street and Manchester Road, boasted a select cafe in addition to filmic fare. In 1929, it introduced Burnley's cinemagoers to a new wonder — talking pictures. Hit by the emergence of mass television ownership in the 1950s, the cinema was demolished to make way for the construction of a new Martin's Bank in the early 1960s — today the location of a discount store. This view dates from 1953.

The existence of the overhead tram cables in this view of St James' Street, Burnley, tells that the picture was taken some time after 1901 when the Corporation began electrification of the steam tramways system they had bought for £53,000 from its private operators. This short, 100-yard length of the town's main-street contained no fewer than five public houses, with the Old Red Lion and the Swan, just out of camera shot at the right, competing with the Clock Face Inn, the White Lion and the Boot Inn for customers. Squeezed in between the pubs were Easton's store — later the location of the highly popular Lubeck Cafe — and, next door, Slater's Tripe, Hot Pies and Pudding Saloon. In addition to its ales, the White Lion advertises good stabling while the typical weaver's cottage windows of the Clock Face, which closed in 1960, point to an ancestry in the hand-loom era. About the time this picture was taken, Burnley had some 300 licensed premises.

St James' Street, Burnley, with the junction with Manchester Road at the left. This scene, captured before the turn of the century, is vastly changed today. Only St James' Hall, the building at the centre of the picture, survives — minus its top storey and clock tower. The Bull Hotel, which was demolished in 1932 and replaced by the Burton's tailor's building at the bottom of Manchester Road, was formerly known as the Black Bull — the spot being listed as the site of an inn as early as 1760. The gas lamp in the middle of the street was nicknamed 'The Gawmless' — a pun referring to its alleged dimness. The lamp was removed in 1920.

Burnley town centre in the 1950s — looking from Yorkshire Street into St James' Street. The white building in the background is that of Burton's tailor's which superseded the Bull Hotel on the site. At the right is the Palace-Hippodrome Theatre which opened in December, 1907. Costing £13,000 and seating 2,000, it served up revues, variety, concerts, cinema and finally bingo before being bulldozed in 1974. The letters 'HG' and 'CW' on the number-plates of the vehicles in the picture identify them as having been registered in Burnley. This spot is now a traffic-free zone.

Standing on the corner of Hall Street, near where Yorkshire Street and St James' Street met — at a spot known as the Top of Wapping, after the thus-named part of the town centre at the bottom of Hall Street — was the Hall Inn. Seen here before the turn of the century, the inn, which got its name from having once been owned by the Towneleys of Towneley Hall, also doubled as a theatre and ballroom in Georgian times. It was later rebuilt in a much more ornate style. Now, the offices of the Norwich Union insurance group occupy the site.

St James' Street, Burnley, in the 1950s — part of the block between Market Street and Chancery Street, all of which disappeared in the 1960s town-centre redevelopment. The public house (left) with the whitened doorstep was the White Horse. Just to the right of the 1864 building housing the Dolcis shoe store and the Wesleyan and General Assurance society — behind whose sign a large clock used to give the time to Burnley folk — stood one of the town's best-loved pubs, the Thorn Hotel, which was erected on the site of a farm about 1740.

St James' Street, Burnley, 1954. The Victoria Theatre and the adjoining Empire Music Hall — the latter seen here as the New Empire cinema — began as places of entertainment in the early 1890s. The Vic, which opened with a performance by the famous Spanish-born opera singer, Madame Patti, was host to many great stars during more than 60 years as a home of live theatre. In 1940, it became the wartime base for London's Old Vic and Sadlers Wells companies.

Closed in March 1955, Burnley's famous 'Vic' theatre in St James' Street is pictured being demolished the following November.

The curtain may have come down on professional theatre in Burnley with the closure of the 'Vic' in 1955, but plays continued to be staged in the town here — in the little Phoenix Theatre over the New Market Hotel in Market Street. The tiny auditorium was taken over in 1929 by the town's amateur dramatics Garrick Club whose productions there always played to members-only full houses. The theatre began life at the start of the century as an old-time music-hall and its boards were trodden by such stars of the day as Little Tich, Dan Leno and George Formby, Senior. Later, it was home to boxing tournaments for several years and afterwards, until it was restored by the Garrick's enthusiasts, it was a warehouse for fish. The Phoenix closed in 1961, with the New Market Hotel being one of the many buildings disappearing in Burnley's central redevelopment.

Burnley's Victorian Market Hall closed in May 1966 — just five months short of the centenary of the laying of its foundation stone in October, 1866. Just how well-built it was is indicated by the fact that more than 10,000 tons of stone went into its construction and that it took until New Year's Day, 1870, before it opened. Little wonder, then, that it at first defied the demolition men's dynamite when its era ended. Burnley's market is among the oldest in the country — its charter having been granted by King Edward I in 1294.

This view of Burnley's outdoor market, taken in 1953, captures all the bustle of the old-time trading spot.

Originally, the town's markets were held near St Peter's Church where a market cross was erected in 1296. The town's new markets opened in November 1969, marking the completion of the first phase of the town's central redevelopment. In the centre of the picture, among the shops on Market Street, is the New Market Hotel where Burnley's unusual Phoenix Theatre was based.

A favourite stop for hungry shoppers on Burnley's old market was this stall, selling black puddings and tripe — for which salt and vinegar seasoning was on hand.

Another view of Burnley market — looking along Howe Street towards Market Street around the turn of the century.

Hargreaves Street, Burnley, *c*.1900 — before the erection of the General Post Office on the right of the street. In the background, in Hammerton Street, are the imposing premises of the town's Co-operative Society. The Co-op had begun in just one shop in Hammerton Street in 1860, but business expanded so rapidly that the society's outlets spread along the street, with extra premises being added in 1885, 1889, 1899 and 1905.

After being abandoned by the Army, Burnley Barracks became home to many former soldiers in a new life as a privately-owned men's lodging house. When this picture was taken in 1967 of their common room, where a coal-fired stove provided heating and cooking facilities, more than half the 55 residents were soldier pensioners. A night's lodging cost four shillings (20 pence).

The Sun Inn now-vanished from town-centre Bridge Street, Burnley, boasted a billiard table among its attractions when this picture was taken about 1910. The date stone above the door was from the year, 1790. Further along the street were the premises of Burnley School of Arms and Gymnasium whose principal was a Mr J.Gorman.

The tower of cotton waste firm John Watts — containing Burnley's first-ever public clock — was a major Burnley landmark and a
key feature of the town's canalside Weaver's Triangle industrial heritage area that recalls Burnley's eminence as one of the major textile
towns of the world — with a peak reached in 1913 when the district clattered to the din of 100,000 looms. Sadly, Clock Tower Mill
was destroyed in huge blaze in 1987. Nearby, stands Slater Terrace, a quaint row of 11 cottages with balconies jutting out over the
canal, built in 1850 by manufacturer George Slater for his key workers at Trafalgar Mill.

Mill chimneys in the Fulledge area of Burnley in 1953 — a view taken through the archway at the Todmorden Road gatehouse to Towneley Hall. Pollution of the air by industry and domestic coal users put Burnley at the top of a national league of soot-smudged towns in 1927. While the government estimated London was covered by 300 tons of soot a year, costing its residents £1.30 a head, in Burnley the amount was nearly three times as great. The lorry in the picture was owned by Padiham Aerated Water Ltd, a minerals drink firm taken over by Burnley's Massey's brewery in 1965.

Towneley Hall, Burnley, 1799 — a copy of a watercolour by J.M.W.Turner as an illustration to the Rev Thomas Dunham Whitaker's *History of Whalley*, the 1800 book which is a bedrock source for all East Lancashire's historians. The ancient hall and 62 acres of grounds, connected with the Towneley family since at least the thirteenth century, were bought by the Corporation in 1902 to become an art gallery and museum, surrounded by a public park.

Duke Bar, Burnley, at the junction of Colne Road and Briercliffe Road, was once known as Hebrew Bar — with Hebrew Road lying nearby. Here, tolls were collected in the turnpike age from Yorkshire-bound traffic. In this 1906 view, an open-top tram is heading for Nelson and a horse-drawn coal cart plods towards Briercliffe. The Duke of York Hotel in the centre was built about 1882, but the building (left), housing Thomas Bate's grocery and 'Duke Bar Bottle Stores', selling Grimshaw's ales, dated from 1858.

Duke Bar, Burnley, looking from Briercliffe Road towards Hebrew Road in the centre of the picture. This view was taken about 1920.

Burnley's original centre — Church Street and, leading off to the right, Godley Lane, pictured in 1880. These old buildings facing St Peter's Church were demolished a year later when Church Street was widened and present-day Ormerod Road was created. The town's ancient market cross and stocks were removed to the nearby grounds of the old Burnley Grammar School. The still-standing row of buildings in the distance, further up Church Street, is dated 1837.

Church Street, Burnley, after the transformation of the town's ancient centre and market place. To the right, opposite St Peter's Church, is the 'new' Talbot Hotel built in 1888. This view dates from 1905.

Pictured in 1896, this is the former head office of the Burnley Building Society in Grimshaw Street. The society, founded in 1850 by a small group of businessmen meeting in a small back room in Market Street, grew to be the largest based in the North West and one of the biggest in the country before merging with the Bradford-based Provincial Building Society in 1982.

In 1929, the Burnley Building Society opened much more imposing headquarters in Grimshaw Street, seen here in the centre of this 1950 view showing the bus station on the town's old Cattle Market. However, by 1964, the society had so outgrown its main accommodation that it trebled the size of head offices with a large extension at the rear. The public house on the corner of Parker Lane, across the road from the building society, was the Rose and Thistle Hotel. In the background can be seen the dome of the Savoy Cinema.

The Cattle Market's service as a bus station site was greatly reduced in 1957 with the erection of the town's new police headquarters and magistrates' court on the site. Burnley's annual summer fair had earlier lost its place there in 1951. Previously, the police and justices' court were located at the back of the Town Hall which opened in Manchester Road in 1888 — its clock tower being visible in the background of this view. The car parking area in the foreground disappeared with the building of the Thompson Recreation Centre on the spot in 1974.

This part of St James' Street, Burnley, seen here about the time of World War One, changed vastly with the demolition in 1973 of the buildings on the left of the roadway — including the town's main Transport Office with its once-familiar clock. The area was also pedestrianised in a 1989 improvement scheme.

Gannow Top, Burnley — where Gannow Lane (left) climbed to join Padiham Road. Seen here in 1963, this area was transformed by the development there in 1979 of the giant interchange with the M65 motorway.

Manchester Road, Burnley, prior to World War One. The building at the right, on the corner of Grimshaw Street, was designed by local architect William Angelo Waddington, who, together with his father, was responsible for the appearance of several banks, churches and local government buildings in Burnley. This one opened in 1894 as the Union Bank, becoming a branch of Barclay's in 1940 before being sold in 1977 to the Burnley Building Society which four years later turned it into a branch office. Now, it houses the Endsleigh insurance centre.

This 1938 view shows the site of Grimshaw's Brewery — the partly demolished building at the right where Burnley's Keirby Hotel now stands. The brewery merged with Massey's in 1928. Opposite is the Well Hall Hotel.

The bottom of Sandygate, Burnley, at its junction with Westgate — an area once known as Whin Hill — in the mid-1920s. The prominent advertisement for Massey's alcoholic beverages no doubt owed much to the firm's brewery being located across the road, a few strides up Westgate. Its closure in 1974, following the acquisition of Massey's by Bass-Charrington eight years earlier, at the time brought an end to at least three centuries of brewing in Burnley. Ironically, the shop at the left of the picture, surrounded by advertisements for strong drink and for the Cross Keys pub in nearby St James' Street, is a temperance bar — owned by herbalist J.Gibbons whose shop-front sign urges: 'Try Our Famous Blood Drink. Always Good.' Next door, to the right, was an eating house, and, in the centre of the row, J.Butler's newsagent's, with Alf Bailey's hairdressing saloon alongside. The shop at the right was a clogger's. Interestingly, it was a confectioner's a little earlier — owned by one Luke Gannon. The same person, one wonders, as the Burnley showman of that name who prised coppers from holidaymakers with his lurid stunts on Blackpool's Golden Mile? For, about the time the shop changed hands, Luke Gannon's exhibitions started at the seaside.

Munn's Corner in St James' Street, Burnley pictured here in 1896, took its name from the premises there of Robert Munn's chemist's and druggist's shop (centre). Mr Munn was also registrar of births, marriages and deaths. Soon after this picture was taken, he took up those duties in nearby Nicholas Street where the town's Register Office is still based. Next door to his shop in St James' Street is Charles Henry Webster's pawnbroker's, while further up the street, with its sign advertising ales and beds is Mrs M.J.Cryer's eating house — located roughly opposite the junction with Parker Lane.

Smaller Towns

Bull Bridge, Accrington, around 1906. The nearby Ye Olde Black Bull pub, from which this spot took its name, was demolished in 1984. A pub was recorded on the site in the early sixteenth century — when this was a crossing point on the River Hyndburn on the main road from Manchester to Whalley. The inn was also the scene of the vestry meetings which ran the town before the organisation of modern-day local government. The Ambulance Drill Hall on the left of the road was opened in 1905 by Boer War hero and founder of the Scout movement, Lord Baden-Powell. It was demolished in 1986.

Bull Bridge, Accrington, in 1902 — before the building of the Ambulance Drill Hall. The town's 21-arch railway viaduct is now a listed structure.

Blackburn Road, Accrington, around 1900. Looking towards the town centre, the row of shops on the block leading to Portland Street still stands. The larger building in the centre of the picture houses Heaton's furniture and floor-coverings shop. Around this time, Accrington Corporation was developing its electricity works whose power was about to spell the demise of the town's 'Baltic Fleet' of steam-hauled trams, like the one seen here trundling towards Church.

Blackburn Road, Accrington, 1913. This stretch between Abbey Street and Peel Street is known locally as Little Blackburn Road. Wardleworth's bookshop, on the right, later moved across the road and the firm still trades in the town centre. The shop on the left of the street, with its owner's sign hanging over the pavement, was that of boot and shoemaker Frederick Augustus Eltoft.

Looking up Little Blackburn Road, from the junction of Peel Street and Church Street, being crossed in this 1896 view by a workman tugging a handcart laden with a barrel. The Cash Clothing Company, on the corner at the left, boasted that it was 'The Largest Clothiers in The World. Branches Everywhere'. Up the street, a flag advertises Abraham Altham's tea. The building at the top of the street, in the centre of the picture, is the Abbey Street branch of the Accrington and Church Industrial Co-operative Society. On the right, near where a web of wrought ironwork hangs over the pavement, can also be seen a large gilded wooden boot, suspended at first-floor level, telling of the existence of Fred Dugdale's shoe shop below, while at the top of the street at the left hangs a huge smoker's pipe belonging to Frederick Royston's tobacconist's. On Church Street, at the right, where two men stand in front of the Commercial Hotel's window, a sign by the doorway announces that the hostelry offers 'An Ordinary Daily at 1pm' — a luncheon of set fare.

This pair of Russian cannons used to stand in Accrington's Oak Hill Park. The park opened in 1893, having cost the Corporation £11,500 when it was bought — at the rate of 1.5 old pence per square foot — from owner from Reginald Gervis Hargreaves, grandson of calico printing pioneer Thomas Hargreaves, who built Oak Hill mansion in its grounds in 1815.

Manchester Road, Accrington, 1928, showing the Wesley Chapel in the background. Plans to include the 1866 chapel as a community centre in a post-war redevelopment scheme never materialised and the building was demolished in the 1960s after its landmark tower became unsafe.

After the building of Accrington's law courts, police and fire station on the site of the old buildings in the foreground of the previous picture, Manchester Road came to look as it did in this 1962 view of the scene. The road opened in 1792. It was the last of the projects carried out by John 'Blind Jack' Metcalf, of Knaresborough, the famous eighteenth-century road builder.

Union Street, Accrington. When this picture was taken in 1961, the street, which took its name from the old workhouse which once stood there, was some 200 years old. The cottage properties on the left were demolished soon afterwards in order to transform the thoroughfare into one of the town's principal shopping streets — a process already under way at the right where new shops and stores are being built in the first phase of the town's central redevelopment.

The sunken gardens on Broadway, Accrington, pictured here in 1958, disappeared soon afterwards when shops and stores were erected on the site. In the background is the Odeon Cinema.

The Big Lamp stood at the top of Deardengate, Haslingden, from 1841. Having survived a plan to remove it in 1926, the lamp was uprooted in 1962 when the Council decided it was a traffic hazard. The lamp, erected by public subscription, was lit by gas supplied free by the old Haslingden Union Gas Company until nationalisation of the industry in 1947. Later, it was converted to electricity. The lamp was bought by a local shoe manufacturer and re-erected in the grounds of his home in Helmshore Road, where it still stands.

December, 1962 — Haslingden's Big Lamp leaves Deardengate after 121 years.

Higher Deardengate, Haslingden, in the 1890s. Cattle and customers mingle on a market day. In the background is the town's Public Hall which was built in 1868. On sale of the traders' stalls in the foreground are piles of that favourite Lancashire delicacy, the black pudding.

Looking down Manchester Road, Haslingden, from the junction with Deardengate. The decorations were part of the town's celebrations for Queen Victoria's jubilee in 1897.

Haslingden Road, Rawtenstall — strung with flags and bunting for the 1902 Coronation of Edward VII. In the background is Haslingden Road Methodist Church which later housed the magistrates' court.

Rawtenstall town centre. This is some time after 1909 when the electrification of the tramways brought the network of overhead wires. The dome of the town's public library is seen at the right. The building was opened in 1906 and officially inaugurated a year later by its donor, the Scots-born American steel magnate, Andrew Carnegie. The Grand Theatre, dominating the scene, was built in 1899 at a cost of £16,000. A few years before its demolition in 1938, it became a cinema — where films were projected on to the back of the screen. The spot was used as a bus station for some time afterwards.

Captain Fold, Rawtenstall. This quaint corner of the town centre, overlooked by Haslingden Road Methodist Chapel, disappeared with the building of the College of Further Education and the Rawtenstall-Edenfield by-pass.

Bank Street, Rawtenstall, c.1911, with the old Lancashire and Yorkshire Bank at the left. The clock overhanging the pavement belonged to the local jewellery firm, Coupe's. It is now on display at the town's Whitaker Museum which acquired it after its original site was pulled down to make way for the new highway.

Rawtenstall Cattle Fair, c.1898. Also known as Rawtenstall May Fair, it was originally held on Tup Meadow, where Hobson Street and Alexandria Street were built a few years later. In the background are the presbytery of St James-the-Less and the church's school. In the distance is the chapel in Rawtenstall cemetery.

Schoolboy cricket being played on waste land — now the library gardens — in front of the Queen's Arms Hotel, Rawtenstall, standing on the corner of Bacup Road (right). This 1895 view also features a steam tram, puffing smoke from its chimney as it travels on the line to Crawshawbooth.

Union Road, Oswaldtwistle, dominated in this 1910 view by the large store of the town's Co-operative Society which had, by then, grown to nearly 1,600 members after being founded in 1866. The days when the society paid them its quarterly dividends were known locally as 'Ossy Races'. So thriving was the Co-op that its dividends grew to as much as 3s 6d in the pound — although a shilling of this was in the form of a voucher.

Oswaldtwistle Town Hall and fire station in Union Road, pictured in 1905. The council offices opened in 1891, by which time the town's population had more than doubled in 50 years to 13,500.

The Black Dog Inn and the Rose and Crown Hotel at the top of Union Road, Oswaldtwistle. This picture was taken some time before 1907 when the spot became a terminus for the new electric trams that linked the town with Accrington.

The Castle Inn in the centre of this turn-of-the-century view of Union Road, Oswaldtwistle, was one of 26 pubs and beerhouses which lined the town's main thoroughfare.

Church Street, Padiham. The white-fronted building on the right of the street was erected in 1610, but was only the Bull Inn from 1899 to 1939 before serving as an Auxiliary Fire Service post during wartime. The Parish Church of St Leonard, next door, dates from 1868, but stands on the site of a medieval chantry.

Down the hill from St Leonard's Church stood Padiham's tramway terminus. Here, a double-decker is destined for Nelson.

The Green, Darwen, showing the town's first model lodging house. The narrow street at the left is Green Street, leading to the Circus. The lodging house stood somewhat further into the Green, towards the White Lion, than the present-day buildings at this spot. Green Street was widened and straightened when the buildings were demolished in the 1920s.

Opposite page: India Mill, Darwen. The giant cotton spinning mill complex, off Bolton Road, took more than 14 years to build before it and its famous chimney, more than 300ft high, was completed in 1867 for owner Eccles Shorrock. It was officially opened in May 1868, by the Marquis of Hartington. The huge block of stone on which the imitation Venetian campanile chimney rests was hewn from a quarry at Cadshaw near the Darwen-Bolton boundary and a team of 35 horses was needed to haul it to the site. It was reputed to be the largest single stone quarried since Cleopatra's Needle. At the time of its completion, the chimney was the tallest and most expensive in the country. It is pictured here with the 14ft-high iron crest which, when it was removed in 1943, provided 20 tons of scrap for the war effort.

Darwen Iron Works. Erected in 1870 adjoining the railway at Goosehouse, with its own large sidings and shunting engine, the works was successively owned by the Darwen Iron Company, Storeys of Lancaster, and the Darwen and Mostyn Iron Company. In 1888, it employed 110 people on an average wage of £1 a week and in later years its workforce was more than 200. Darwen people used to set their clocks by its 10pm works siren. Slack trade after World War One led to a series of long stoppages and temporary resumptions before the works closed in 1927. Its 200ft-high iron chimney and glare from the furnace provided a spectacle each night. Demolition of the plant began in May 1936.

The original caption on this picture says, 'Darwen Station 40 Years Ago.' But although there is no knowing when it was taken, judging from the appearance of the locomotive, with its completely-exposed footplate, and that of the bystanders, it cannot have been too long after the opening through Darwen of the Manchester-Blackburn rail link in 1848. One wonders whether the two youngsters wearing soldier-style suits is a clue to the period being that of the 1853-56 Crimean War in which Britain was embroiled.

The Victoria Tower, Darwen. Standing 1,225ft above sea level, the 86ft landmark was the town's tribute to Queen Victoria's Diamond Jubilee in June 1897, with £700 being raised for its construction by public donations. It took more than a year to build, with the official opening by the Lord of the Manor, the Rev W.A.Duckworth, taking place on 24 September 1898, when this huge celebration bonfire was lit. The metal and glass dome at the top of the tower was blown off in a gale in 1947 and replaced by a replica in 1972.

The 'new' Darwen Station was built in 1883-84 at the top of Railway Road.

1902 and decorations for the Coronation of Edward VII deck town-centre Market Street, Darwen, and the Angel Inn in the centre of the picture. Underneath the giant crown which has been fixed for the occasion to the now-vanished pub at first-floor level is a sign, telling that the landlord was Samuel Rawlinson. The Angel sold beer supplied by Dutton's Brewery at Blackburn. What appears to be a large slot machine for the sale of cigars can be seen to the left of the pub's doorway.

Green Street, Darwen, 1904, with the Angel Inn (right) at the junction with Market Street. The pub seems to be receiving a delivery at its side door, with a cart belonging to Medico Ltd, a chemists and mineral water manufacturers based in Pump Street, Blackburn. Just up the street, on the right, is Walter Roan's shop, selling saddlery and trunks and just beyond are the premises of plumber Edward Wrighton. The draper's shop in the foreground (left) is also a receiving office for the Rosehill Laundry at Blackburn. All the buildings in Green Street were demolished in the 1920s in the Lumb Street, Water Street and Green Street clearance.

Although dated 1904, the decorations suggest that this picture of Church Street, Darwen, was probably taken two years earlier — at the time of King Edward VII's Coronation. The Manchester and County Bank on the corner with Market Street at the left is now the National Westminster. At the right, on the corner with Bridge Street, is the Millstone Hotel. Next door, is a barber's shop and, just beyond, the shop of chemist William Henry Lomax while, at the other end of the building, near where a horse and cart stand, a sign at first-floor level indicates the headquarters of Darwen Cycling Club. Further up the street, in the vicinity of the Central Conservative Club, some work at the top of a ladder is attracting attention. More flags fly from the tower of Holy Trinity Church, which was built in 1827-29 with a parliamentary grant of £6,799 from the £1 million fund set up by the government in thanksgiving for the defeat of Napoleon at Waterloo. The public clock was added to the tower in 1878 and Holy Trinity changed its name to St Peter's in 1974 when the parish was merged with those of St John and St George.

Darwen's old open-air market place. The town's three-day market went 'indoors' when a new covered complex opened on the square in 1975. It replaced the open-sided wooden-roofed structure under which traders later gathered when they abandoned their more flimsy stalls, some of which are seen without their canvas awnings in this turn-of-the-century view which also features a swinging-boat amusement ride. The Market Hall at the right was built in 1881-82 and also housed the town's municipal offices. The clock in its tower was added in 1900 — a £150 gift of Dr James Todd Ballantyne, as a memento of his year as mayor.

Bolton Road, Darwen, near the Old Belgrave Mills on the left — a view taken some time after 1900 when the town's trams, one of which is seen in the distance, began to run on electricity drawn from the overhead power lines. Tram services ceased on the Circus-Whitehall route along Bolton Road in March 1940, despite wartime fuel shortages having led to them briefly being reinstated after they were first withdrawn in January 1939. Darwen's last tram ran on 5 October 1946 — on the Circus-Blackburn Boundary route.

The Towngate, Great Harwood — a view, believed to date from the 1880s, taken from Church Street, looking towards the site now occupied by the National Westminster Bank building and the former Urban District Council offices, which opened in 1900. By then, Elias Berry had moved his ironmongery business to two premises in Queen Street around the corner. Among the implements on sale at his old shop here are hay rakes and forks, a scythe, horse collars and a tin tub. And the wares he advertises include spades, pickaxes, grates, fenders and kitchen ranges. To the right, in the shop with a gable above its first-floor window, is a barber's.

Queen Street, Great Harwood, at the junction with Church Street. The stone steps behind the gas lamp on the corner at the left were known as 'Todd's Steps' — no doubt referring to ironmonger Joseph William Todd whose premises were at Nos. 1 and 3 Queen Street.

Hay, straw and corn dealer Thomas Hanson supplied feed for all kinds of animals as the advertisements on his shop, standing at the corner of St Hubert's Street and Over Street, Great Harwood, testify. In 1900, his business had been located in Queen Street and this picture seems to have been taken in the early 1920s after a change of premises.

The Market Hall and Library, Nelson, 1890 — a view down Market Street to Cross Street. Built the previous year, the Market Hall accommodated the Public Library from April 1890 until 1895 when its books were transferred to the newly-built Technical School. The clock tower, which was added to the building in 1904, was one of the few things left standing when fire swept the Market Hall in March 1932. Nelson's Library was built on the site in 1974.

Nelson centre, *c*.1900, looking from Manchester Road down Scotland Road, with the Lord Nelson Hotel at the left. William Widdup's furniture store, advertised on the corner building behind the ornate drinking fountain and lamp, was located further down Scotland Road on the left. Tom Forsyth's hatter's and hosier's shop had been located at No.1 Leeds Road for about five years when this picture was taken. Manley and Hartley's shop, on the corner of Market Street and Scotland Road (left) was an ironmonger's and mill furnisher's.

Nelson town centre in the early 1950s. The Barclays Bank building, with its distinctive clock tower, is now occupied by the National and Provincial Building Society. Erected just before World War One for the Union Bank of Manchester, the building's clock tower was altered in 1955 when the dome was encased in an aluminium 'helmet' and its weather vane was removed. The clock was maintained by the Town Council.

Manchester Road, Nelson, at the time this pre-World War One picture was taken echoed to the rattle of trams along the tracks and the slower-paced rumble of cart wheels over its countless setts.

Clitheroe, looking up Wellgate towards the Market Place. This picture is dated about 1905. It was in October of that year that the town's Carnegie Library at the junction with Church Street was opened. It is seen here with its clock tower nearing completion. The little girl in the foreground was, as Mrs J.Entwistle, to be Clitheroe's mayoress 55 years later. The cab at the left of the street probably belonged to undertaker and cab proprietor James Garlick whose business was in Wellgate Mews. At the right, is a butcher's cart while in the foreground is the shop of boot and shoe maker James Smalley. The barber's pole is outside Daniel Wrigley's shop.

The Market Place, Clitheroe, before the building of the Carnegie Library at the junction of Church Street (left) and York Street. On the site of the library stands Bailey Brothers' corn miller's and grocer's shop. Behind, marked by its tower, is the Town Hall, built in 1822. In front of the shop, seen to the right of its doorway, is a drinking fountain. At the near right is the Brownlow Arms Hotel and in the distance at the corner of York Street and Wellgate is the Dun Horse Inn.

A 1930s view of Clitheroe's Market Place, with the old drinking fountain and the Dun Horse Inn gone.

This view of Clitheroe's Norman Castle, whose actual age is lost in antiquity, shows Castle Street and the buildings beneath the keep about 1900.

Clitheroe town centre in the 1920s — looking from the Market Place towards the castle.

St James' Street, Bacup, 1900, looking in the direction of Rochdale.

Bacup town centre — looking towards Irwell Terrace in the background from the location of present-day St James' Square. The Conservative Club near the centre of the picture, next to the Weavers' Association offices, had its top storey removed in 1960s because of dry rot. At the right, behind the horse and cart, is the Golden Lion pub.

Market Street, Bacup, in the 1930s, looking towards the town centre, with the King George V Hotel on the corner of Burnley Road. All the property on the right has since been demolished. On the right at the corner of Tower Street is an Altham's tea store, once a familiar feature of most East Lancashire towns, but now better known as a travel agency business.

Bacup town centre in the late nineteenth century. Behind the low wall at the end of the street, the River Irwell was still exposed to view. Irwell Terrace in the distance awaits the construction in 1893 of the Conservative Club. The large building in the centre is the Mechanics' Hall.

Colne, 1912 — a view from Mill Green, Waterside, an area of the town which contained a dozen mills. On the right of the picture is the Admiral Lord Rodney Inn, named after the hero of a great naval victory over the French in 1782.

Colne & District Co-operative Society's central premises in Albert Road opened in 1907. It was the first department store in England to use steel-reinforced concrete in its construction.

An electric tramcar on Albert Road, Colne. Public transport at first consisted of two horse-drawn buses which travelled to and from Trawden. But at the turn of the century, the town acquired six 50-seater electric tramcars. Trams finally ran in Colne in January 1934, by when it was estimated they had travelled more than 4.5 million miles, carried 57.5 million passengers and consumed 9.5 million units of electricity. In the background of this view is Colne Town Hall which opened in 1894.

Colne's market is believed to have been well established long before the first record of its existence in 1588. Seen here in Market Street, it was last held in the main thoroughfare in 1897 by when the growth in population and traffic made it too much of an obstruction. The 'new' market with its covered Market Hall built on Skelton Field below Dockray Street was formally opened in March 1898. On the left of this view stands the Black Bull Hotel and the gable with a rectangular chimney near the centre of the picture is that of the Swan Hotel. So thriving was the market that more than a dozen inns and taverns flanked it.

Cattle in the street were a common sight on market days in nineteenth-century Colne.

A sunny day in Colne Lane in 1922. The girls' dresses suggest that their destination might have been a church 'walking day'.

Villages

The mill village of Goodshawfold, near Loveclough in Rossendale, acquired its unusual 'Spewing Duck' water trough and spring in 1855 after the money for it was provided by public subscription and the executors of the late John Hargreaves. The well's nickname referred to its original spout, shaped like a duck's neck.

Higham on the southern slopes of Pendle Hill, near Burnley, regained some of the tranquillity of this 1947 view when the opening of the Padiham by-pass in 1969 removed much of the traffic from its main street. The village's two cotton mills, opened in 1850, employed the majority of its population.

Stopper Lane, Rimington, in the Ribble Valley, showing what is believed to be one of the last windmills in Ribblesdale, in use as a saw mill in the 1920s before it was demolished.

Mellor, near Blackburn. The water supply was a long-standing problem for the hilltop community which was forced to rely on wells and springs until the formation in 1902 of the village's own water company relieved many of the residents from the drudgery of carrying buckets to and fro. It sank a borehole on Mellor Moor, near the Jinny Spring, one of the wells that Mellor folk — known locally as 'polts' — depended on. The windmill pumping station filled a small reservoir which was originally connected to 100 properties. But residents at the top end of the village, whose homes were higher than the level of the reservoir, were still forced to carry water as much as a mile. The water company was taken over by Blackburn's undertaking in 1952.

Mellor Brook, with the Feilden Arms pub at the left and, behind the pony and trap, the entrance to Mellor Brow. This tranquil scene was transformed into a busy — and dangerous — spot when the arrival of vehicles turned the country lane seen here into the A59 major route from Liverpool to Yorkshire. Peace was restored in 1992 with the opening of the by-pass around the village. In the distance are the chimney of Elswick Mill and the spire of St Mary's Church at Mellor.

The Five Barred Gate Hotel, standing at the junction of the A59 and the A677 on the western approach to East Lancashire at Samlesbury, took its name from the old toll gate close by. Seen here with a row of thatched cottages adjoining, the pub disappeared in 1960 when it fell in the path of the new dual carriageway that was built to the M6 motorway. Before it was demolished, it was replaced by a much larger public house built nearby which was expanded to become a luxury hotel and renamed as the Trafalgar Hotel in the 1970s.

This picture, taken on 1 November 1890, at the old Shackerley Toll Bar near the Blackburn boundary on Preston New Road at Mellor, marked the end of an era in road travel in Lancashire. At midnight on 31 October, tolls were ended on the road and at the county's two other remaining toll bars — at Nine Ash and Brockholes Bridge, also on the Blackburn-Preston road. The road, which had been a turnpike since 1826, came under the control of Lancashire County Council and travel along it became 'free to the public for ever'.

Paris, Ramsgreave, near Blackburn. The row of handloom weavers' cottages, built in 1841-42, were once also known as Paris Houses. But their association with the 'naughty' French capital came about because the women living there — many of whom were married — supplemented their income from weaving by engaging in part-time prostitution. The cottages became called 'Little Paris', although the prefix had been dropped by the time of the 1851 census.

Knowsley Road, Wilpshire, leading to the area known locally as Wilpshire Bottoms, was a quiet country lane passing beneath the Blackburn-Hellifield line when this picture was taken. Now, it is an access-only road to prevent it being used by motorists as a 'rat run' to avoid the traffic lights at the Whalley New Road-Ribchester Road junction.

Copster Green, near Blackburn, was also unofficially known as 'Goose Muck Hillock' after the farmyard fowl found around the now-vanished pond on the village's common. Working folk from Blackburn visited the spot for picnics and outings at weekends in the years before World War Two, trekking there from the tram terminus at Wilpshire for a breath of country air and refreshments sold to them by the villagers.

Beyond the reach of town trams and the railway, the Ribble Valley village of Ribchester, famous for the remains of its Roman fort, was a popular destination for cyclists. This spot, near the churchyard on the banks of the River Ribble, was where a Roman pillar was found in September 1904. On the right is the village's old schoolhouse and the farm building in the background is being converted into a house.

The De Tabley Arms, Clayton-le-Dale, pictured here in the early 1900s, stands on the bank of the Ribble near Ribchester Bridge and, until some 70 years earlier, was known as the Bridge Inn. It changed its name after Lord De Tabley inherited the local Talbot estates. The inn became a night club in 1983.

Christ Church, Chatburn, was seriously damaged by lightning on 3 May 1854. Built in 1837, it is believed to be the first church constructed during the reign of Queen Victoria.

Holme-in-Cliviger, 1887. On the right is the Ram Inn and, glimpsed through the gateway at the left, is St John's Church. Consecrated in 1794, it was founded by Dr Thomas Dunham Whitaker, East Lancashire's most important local historian, whose family history can be traced back at Holme to 1431. After his death at Blackburn in 1821, he was buried in the family vault at St John's. Also interred in the graveyard are General Sir James Yorke Scarlett, hero of the siege of Balaclava in the Crimean War, and Lady O'Hagan, the last of the Towneley family to live at Towneley Hall, Burnley. The schoolhouse (far left), erected by Dr Whitaker about 1819, has since been rebuilt and the cottage (centre) stands where the village war memorial was placed. The village stocks can be glimpsed at left of the cottage's gable end, by the woman in a light-coloured dress.

Hilltop Newchurch-in-Rossendale is credited with being the valley's oldest village. This is a view of Church Street about 1900 — a spot much altered by clearance and rebuilding in the early 1960s. Once a key point on the route from Rochdale to Whalley before it was bypassed by the cutting of a more convenient road out of the valley floor, the village first got the church from which it draws its name in 1511. Originally a chapel of ease to Whalley, it was rebuilt in 1561, 1753 and to its present form in 1824.

Burnley Road, Lumb, about 1920, with Dean Lane at the left.

Crankshaw Corner, Burnley Road, Crawshawbooth, took its name from the grocer's shop near the centre of this early 1900s view. It disappeared when the road was widened and straightened at this spot — a move which also swept away the old Manchester and County Bank at the far left and the original Black Dog Hotel, standing behind the gas lamp at the right. However, Rawstron's 'Paris House' — the building at the centre with the arched, second-floor window — and the properties to its right survived.

Waterfoot 1891. The market building, standing alongside J.Richardson's boot, shoe and clog maker's shop, by the big lamp at the junction of Bacup Road and Burnley Road, disappeared with the arrival in 1899 of the shopping arcade that was the brainchild of footwear manufacturer Sir Henry Trickett. A crowd of 15,000 gathered for the opening ceremony — as Rossendale's MP, J.H.Maden, opened the main gates with a golden key. Trickett's Arcade was the only concern in the valley to produce its own electricity and the generator was housed in one of the shop windows for all to see — all a far cry from the 'Newmarket' we see here.

Narrowgates Cottages, Barley, about the turn of the century. Work for the residents of this row, standing in the shadow of Pendle Hill's big end, came from nearby Narrowgates Mill which picturesque Pendle Water helped to run. It survived the 1881 deluge which washed away Barley's other mill, but closed in 1967 after being owned and run for more than 50 years by the Metcalfe family. Seven cottages in Narrowgates were renovated by Pendle Council in 1976 and let to tenants who enjoyed bathrooms, indoor toilets and central heating — luxuries that the villagers here might only have dreamed about.

Roughlee Pleasure Ground, on the slopes of Pendle, near Barrowford, in the 1920s. The mill yard in the village centre joined the amusement industry when loomer and twister Alfred Waine bought a rowing boat in 1912 and launched it on the mill lodge which used to run a water-wheel that was believed to be the second-biggest in the country. The business grew — so that, by the 1950s, it included 12 boats, animals, swinging boats and weekend holiday chalets and caravans. The swinging boats were removed in 1974 after they became unsafe. After changing ownership and becoming run down, the site was bought by Pendle Council in 1989 and turned into a community centre.

The crossroads at Haggate, Briercliffe, with the Sun Inn on Burnley Road at the far left and Kenyon's grocer's on the next corner. Beyond is Haggate Baptist Church whose Sunday School celebrated its centenary in 1983.

Brierfield centre in the early 1900s, with a tramcar on Colne Road departing from the junction with Railway Street at the left.

Langho. The Ribble Valley village grew up around Spring Mill whose chimney valley scrapes the sky at the right of the picture. Opposite these terraced houses was farmland, now occupied by bungalows. The cotton mill was demolished to make way for the opening, in 1970, of a new public house named after the old weaving shed — a move which brought about the closure of the old Langho Hotel, seen in the distance at the centre of the picture. At the far right is the Langho Methodist Church which was erected in 1912, but had to wait until 1937 for the benefit of electric light. The attire of the youngsters in this 1913 view suggests that the picture was taken on a Sunday when the wearing of best clothes was customary.

Belthorn. The moorland village near Blackburn developed in the late eighteenth century when many handloom weavers' cottages were built. The village acquired two cotton mills in the middle of the last century which ceased production in 1933 and 1958 after being the community's major employers. This pre-World War One view, looking down Belthorn Road towards Rann and Blackburn, shows a couple in typical working-class dress. The man is holding a billy-can. At the right is the chimney of Syke Mill. About this time, Belthorn boasted four beerhouses and three public houses.

High Street, Rishton, looking in the direction of Blackburn, c.1904. The village's population was about 8,000, having increased ten-fold since the middle of the previous century as industry in the form of nine cotton mills, coal mining, brick and papermaking expanded an economy once based largely on hand-loom weaving — a craft which lasted until 1874 in Rishton. At the left of the street, beyond the clock overhanging the pavement, is the forecourt of the Roebuck pub which was used as a market site.

Rishton Parish Church — without its Gothic tower. Dedicated to St Peter and Paul, it was consecrated in 1877, but it was not until 1904 that the tower was extended to its full height of some 100ft. Its clock and peal of bells were added a year later. Before the church was built, the school-church in nearby Harwood Road was used for services and, previously, a group of cottages known as the Flats and a room above a smithy near the junction with Harwood Road and Blackburn Road had served as the village's church.

King Street, Whalley, *c.*1900. The Whalley Arms, built in 1781 in the ancient abbey village on the banks of the River Calder, still stands, but the half-timbered building beyond has disappeared. At the right, the Dog Inn, is advertising Cunningham's ales and stout, brewed at the Snig Brook Brewery in Blackburn.

This view of Whalley from Accrington Road comes from a 1900 album compiled by Darwen's Spring Vale Ramblers. On the left, are the village's modern assembly rooms which opened the previous year. Now, they house a nightclub and Whalley Conservative Club. The houses on Queen Street, glimpsed at the far left, are no longer open to view from this spot, another terrace having been built opposite them. The white-painted cottage at the right was one of the three toll-bar houses that levied travellers to and from Whalley on the turnpike era's highways. The oldest stood at the top of Accrington Road, near present-day Whalley Golf Club — the Accrington-Whalley road having been turnpiked in 1789. Later, the bar was removed to the bottom of the brow — to the spot in this picture. Another toll house stood on the new Clitheroe-Whalley road when it was turnpiked about 1809. It was demolished in 1955. In the distance is the tower of Whalley's ancient parish church whose origins reach back to the sixth century.

The Tanners' Arms, Dinckley. Although undated, this picture obviously stems from the early age of motoring. This unusual car has a seat for a passenger facing the driver. In those days, when one James Wilson was licensee, the Tanners' was a remote country beerhouse — a haunt for farmers and travellers taking the nearby ferry across the River Ribble to Hurst Green. This group could hardly have imagined that the arrival of the motoring age would, some 80 years later, turn the place into a Chinese restaurant for those out for a spin and a meal.

Hurst Green — a picture from the 1900 album, compiled by the members of the men's Bible class at Spring Vale Methodist Church at Darwen which formed a rambling club in 1897. This view shows the hub of the picturesque Ribble Valley village before the roads were properly paved — an ironic lack since the famous public school of Stonyhurst College nearby lays claim to having the world's first macadamed road. The patch of grass in the foreground has now been turned into a formal garden. The road in the background leads to Lower Hodder Bridge and Whalley and, on its right, at the centre of the picture, stands the Eagle and Child Hotel.

The picturesque Ribble Valley village of Waddington — a frequent winner of best-kept village contests — did not officially belong to East Lancashire until 1974 when local government reform removed it from Yorkshire. In the background is the parish church of St Helen's.

The Moorcock Inn on the slopes of Waddington Fell grew into one of the best known country inns in the Ribble Valley, with ballroom, restaurant and hotel facilities. Here, judging from the hens in the foreground, the Moorcock, like many country pubs of the period, may also have been a farm. The sign above the door indicates that 'Seedall's Fine Home Brewed Ales and Porter' may have been brewed on the premises, but the different surname of the landlord, William Atkinson, puts this in doubt.

The stream running through the lovely Ribble Valley village of Pendleton no longer has quite the same potential that it had in this view to flood the cottages flanking it. Now, it is contained inside a walled channel. At the left, by the footbridge, is the Swan with Two Necks pub — a name believed to be a corruption of 'nicks', or the marks, made in the beaks of swans to denote their breed or ownership.

The historic village of Downham is often described as the prettiest in Lancashire — and, as such, has long attracted tourists. Seen here, in the 1930s, the village's main street is crowded with visitors, many of them ramblers wearing knapsacks. The bare trees and preponderance of overcoats suggest that this might have been a Good Friday when the sun failed to shine. In the background can be seen the village church, with a tower dating from the fifteenth century, in which hang three bells which used to call the monks at Whalley Abbey to prayer.

Entitled 'Tram Terminus, Cherry Tree', this picture dates from after October 1903, when the tramway line reached this point on Preston Old Road on the outskirts of Blackburn. Previously, the line, opened in 1889 with horse trams, reached only to Witton Stocks. The row of houses on the right, at the junction with Green Lane, was extended in 1902, according to a plaque placed on it, but none of the newer houses is visible yet in this view. The site of the trees further down the road is now the block of houses and shops between Feniscliffe Drive and Cecilia Road. In the background, to the right of the trees, can be glimpsed to former vicarage of St Francis, Feniscliffe. The tram route to Cherry Tree was converted to buses in April, 1939.

Preston Old Road, Cherry Tree. Cattle amble down what is now a busy highway under the arches of Feniscliffe Bridge that carried the Blackburn-Chorley rail link. The branch line, running from Cherry Tree to Adlington, opened in 1869. Passenger services ended in 1960 with goods services from Chorley to Feniscowles continuing until 1966 and the final section between Cherry Tree and Feniscowles closing two years later.

Social

Old-time sanitation in back-street Colne. Once a week, the ash-middens and outdoor privvies in the back yards of the rows of terraced houses were emptied. The unpleasant task of disposing of the waste in privvies' tubs fell to these workmen — the euphemistically-named 'night soil' men. As the name implied, the work was usually carried out at night. Here, one of the workmen is emptying one of the tubs into the horse-drawn tank. Not surprisingly, his ladle has an extremely long handle! Afterwards, the men spread lime to combat disease.

Pendleton, 1903, and villagers celebrate the end of the Boer War — somewhat late as the South African conflict had ended in May the previous year. The group, gathered outside the Swan with Two Necks, included at least four generations of villagers. The bowler-hatted man at the far right is believed to be wearing a medal awarded in the Crimean War of 50 years before and the young boy in front of him is thought to be wearing his father's Boer War medal. The pub's licensee, William Stratton, sold the hostelry shortly after this picture was taken.

A military funeral for a caretaker. July 1901 and Blackburn is brought to a standstill for the passing of Royal Artillery veteran, Sergeant Major John Bedingfield, whose flag-draped coffin is borne on the barrel of a giant field-gun towards the town's cemetery. The part-time soldiers of the 3rd Lancashire Artillery Volunteers organised this splendid send-off for the man who looked after their barracks in King Street, after he died of pneumonia, aged 47. Until three months before, however, Sgt-Major Bedingfield, had served for seven years as an instructor to the Blackburn-based gun corps' five batteries. A soldier since 1873, he had previously served in Afghanistan and Egypt. The picture shows his coffin and funeral procession passing from Church Street, with the White Bull Hotel at the right, towards Salford Bridge.

Best clothes, bowlers and bonnets. These Rossendale folk are all dressed up, with somewhere to go. The five-carriage event is thought to be a works outing from the footwear factory of J.H.Hirst at Waterfoot, but the date, location and occasion are all uncertain.

Oswaldtwistle, 1905, and ten days of non-stop sermon, song and fun are offered by the town's principal Methodist Church, the Mount Pleasant Wesleyan Chapel — even if the unsmiling faces of this group outside the church do not quite pass on the 'Merrie Meeting' message of their placards. The star of the occasion — thought to be the top-hatted man in the doorway — is Josiah Nix, 'Founder of the Racecourse Missions'. Now, the 1846 church in Chapel Street is known as Rhyddings Methodist Church and only a portion remains of the backdrop to this picture. Dry rot led to the demolition of all but a piece of the chapel's frontage which was incorporated in a new church in 1984.

20 June 1903 — Great Harwood honours its famous son, John Mercer, the once-illiterate bobbin boy who invented and gave his name
to 'Mercerised' cotton . . .cloth given a silk-like sheen by the process which Mercer (1791-1866) discovered by accident while experimenting
with caustic soda. The clock tower memorial to him was erected on Great Harwood's Towngate by public subscription and unveiled
by Alderman Thomas Broughton, the Mayor of Accrington.

A man with a mission. The minister of Oswaldtwistle's Mount Pleasant Wesleyan Chapel bangs the drum for his church's 'Merrie Meeting' in 1905.

A swimming class at Blackburn's now-vanished Freckleton Street baths — a picture recalling the era of full-length swimming costumes and the tie-on cotton trunks provided by the council. At the right is Harry Ward, who was swimming instructor at the baths until 1938. He gained fame in the 1900s as a local comedian and top open-water swimmer — training in the town's Queen's Park lake for then-popular mile races in rivers like the Thames and Mersey. Opened in 1868, Freckleton Street boasted two plunges, but things were still a squeeze for the town's swimmers until the opening of Belper Street baths in 1906 alleviated the space problem.

Rossi's hot potato cart, pictured in the 1940s, was a familiar sight for a good 40 years outside the Adelphi Hotel on Blackburn Boulevard. Francis Rossi, seen here by his cart's coal-burning oven, moved to Blackpool in 1952 to run landau rides up and down the promenade after half a lifetime serving twopenny bags of roasted potatoes. He was head of a family familiar to generations of Blackburn people — his father, Joseph, who came from Genoa in Italy, being well-known for his pony and trap ice cream cart, ornately decorated with the crest of the House of Savoy. Tony, the hot potato cart pony, lived for an amazing 40 years.

Polly, the Welsh bay mare, lived an incredible 42 years. She and the delivery van belonged to the Old Country Laundry in Grant Street — now Grant Road — at Witton, Blackburn. When pictured in 1928, they had just won the prize for the best-turned-out horse and van at the Royal Lancashire Show, held that year for the first time in Blackburn — at the Old Mother Redcap. Far right is the company's head van man, Mr Robert Wilkinson with his colleagues Albert Lancaster (left) and Jimmy Pomfret.

Burnley had numerous cycling clubs in 1889 when the camera caught members of the town's Zingari Cycling Club at rest. The club's name — Italian for 'gypsies' — no doubt referred to the desire of its members to wander freely where they pleased. The giant penny-farthing — or Ordinary — bicycle was coming to the end of the road as a popular machine about this time, being superseded by bikes with same-size wheels, powered by the then newly-invented chain drive. The 'modern' machines seen here have foot rests attached to the front forks, showing that the rear-hub free-wheel device which made life safer for riders on downhill descents had yet to arrive on the cycling scene.

This blacked-up comic minstrel band was aboard one of the 40 floats which took part in the 11th annual Rose Queen procession of St James' Church, Clayton-le-Moors, in June 1912. Here, they seem to be heading down Blackburn Road towards the Dunkenhalgh where the crowning of council chairman's daughter Jeannie Clegg took place. A record £60 was collected from the crowd — the proceeds being for a new classroom at St James' school.

A housemaid's big day — Darwen, 1904. This was the town's first wedding car. The bride was Welsh lass, Annie McNamara, who worked as a servant for Darwen mill owner Alec Eccles. For her big day, her boss lent her his motor car and his home — the now-vanished Grange at Hollins Grove — for the reception. She wed local lad Sammy Catterall, who kept wicket for Blackburn's East Lancashire Cricket Club for 21 years. Separated by a bridesmaid, the couple are pictured in the back seat of the car.

Whalley, 1902, and the staff of the village's post office, based in Alfred Camm's chemist's shop in Park Villas, King Street, pose for their picture. Resplendent in their Royal Mail uniforms and shako helmets are four of the five postmen Mr Camm had at his command, along with the two telegraph messengers. In 1901, when Whalley's population was 1,098, they delivered 15,650 parcels and 2,489 telegrams.

A dry run at Stonefold Church of England Primary School, Rising Bridge, as pupils practise swimming without water. The school's most famous son is former Education Minister, Sir Rhodes Boyson, a pupil from 1929 to 1935.

The knocker-up — with his wire-tipped pole that rattled bedroom windows — played a vital role in rousing weavers and factory hands in time for work. Being late for work could result in an employee being sent home and losing a day's pay — or even the sack. The starting time at East Lancashire's mills was 6am, so the knocker-up, like this one at Burnley, had to be an even earlier riser to commence his rounds. The reduction of the working day and the affordability of alarm clocks had by the 1930s greatly reduced the numbers of these once-familiar characters, many of whom were retired mill workers. Reporting the death in 1937 of one of the last of the breed in Blackburn, the old *Northern Daily Telegraph* told of his diligence — in whacking with a hammer at the front doors of those who failed to respond to his window rattling!

'Waste Not, Want Not' is the edifying motto carved on the mantelpiece of the oven range in the kitchen of Blackburn Orphanage where two youngsters apply jam to doorstep-size slices of bread. The orphanage, erected at Wilpshire, was founded by Scottish joiner James Dixon, who began the fund for it in 1886 with his life savings of £50 after finding half a dozen boys sleeping rough in the doorway of a Blackburn warehouse.

The headwear of these coopers and other workers, believed to be at Dutton's Brewery at Salford, Blackburn, suggests that the picture was taken some time in the 1870s.

This car park at the rear of Bolton Road, Ewood, could, according to the sign at the left, accommodate 200 vehicles. Here, it is filled to capacity as a match takes place at nearby Blackburn Rovers' ground in the 1920s.

A turn-of-the-century horse and cart turn-out for the wares of Colne fruit preserver Caleb Duckworth. After leaving Rimington at the age of 14 in 1869, Caleb found work in Colne with William Pickles Hartley, who later earned a knighthood and fame as Europe's biggest producer of preserves. But Caleb resisted Hartley's move in 1874 to a massive new factory at Bootle, near Liverpool, and set up on his own after buying his former employer's dry-salting business which was based in Colne's Piece Hall. In 1894, he designed and produced the first machine for cleaning and de-stalking currants and sultanas, turning it into a world-wide seller and diversifying the business into making machinery for the food and dairy trade — a sector on which it solely concentrated from 1965. The firm also ran a printing business for a time and one of its employees was Philip Snowden, who became Chancellor of the Exchequer in Ramsay MacDonald's Labour government in 1923. Caleb Duckworth's factory closed in Colne in 1986.

This Blackburn Rovers' fan and mascot were dressed up for the team's victorious trip to the 1928 FA Cup Final.

Watched by a crowd of thousands, the official opening of Clitheroe's public library took place on 21 October 1905. The ceremony was to have been performed by Lord Shuttleworth, of Gawthorpe, former MP for the Clitheroe Division, but, because of his absence abroad, Town Clerk John Eastham stood in. Scots-born American tycoon and philanthropist Andrew Carnegie gave £3,000 for the new building which took more than a year to complete. Previously, the town's library occupied the ground floor of the adjoining Town Hall in Church Street. The library movement in Clitheroe went back to the founding of the Mechanics' Institute in 1837, but, in 1844, its library closed and the library moved to the front room of a house in Parson Lane until the Corporation adopted the Free Libraries Act in 1878.

Fire at India Mill, Darwen, 15 June 1908 — sequel to a freak accident. Three days earlier, the mill has been 'bombed' by a flying boiler. The 8cwt vertical boiler was being used for pumping water at the nearby Dimmocks Mill of the Darwen Paper Company when, in the early hours of the previous Friday, it exploded and flew an estimated 200ft into the air before crashing through the roof of India Mill and ending up on the sixth storey where it smashed a spinning mule. The following Monday, half an hour after workmen, who were repairing the roof, had finished for the day, tar they were using caught fire. Mill workers tackled the blaze with hoses until the fire brigade arrived. The firemen built a temporary hoist of trestles, planks and ropes to raise buckets of sand to the roof and extinguished the fire in three-quarters of an hour. The burning tar caused tremendous clouds of smoke, but the fire was more spectacular than serious — damage was actually slight.

This rustic, summerhouse-style building with its leaded, stained-glass windows, standing at the corner of Preston New Road and Billinge Road, Blackburn, was a telephone kiosk belonging to the National Telephone Company. It was sufficiently unusual for it to be featured in 1907 in the company's journal which described it as being not only picturesque, but also an excellent revenue-earner and educator of the public in the use of the telephone. Admission was gained by placing a penny in the coin-operated door mechanism. The town's police, however, had free access — in return for keeping an eye on the place. And, on the first Sunday the call box came into use, they turfed out four fellows they found making use of its table and chairs to play cards and enjoy a quiet smoke. The furniture was duly removed to prevent a recurrence of such behaviour. The kiosk was also equipped with electric lighting and the clock above its door was used by tramcar crews arriving at the nearby Billinge terminus to keep to their schedules.

The first Sunday in August marked the anniversary of Skipton Road Chapel, Trawden — an event known as 't'Sermons'. Here the band, with Hartley Bannister playing the double bass, accompanies the villagers' hymn-singing in 1905.

Darwen, 18 April 1898 — and Lancashire's upper crust goes home after a splendid breakfast. The procession, heading down Bolton Road towards the Circus, was made up of the coaches and carriages of the 'large number of gentlemen of the county' whom Lancashire's recently-appointed High Sheriff, Mr W.B.Huntington, had entertained with a morning repast in a large marquee erected in the grounds of his home, Woodlands, in the Whitehall area of Darwen. Mayors, magistrates, MPs, clergymen and the sheriff's personal friends made up the gathering which was entertained by the band of the Rifle Volunteers. Here, a mayoral coach passes by James Gibson's ironmonger's, with, futher up the street, Thomas Lawless' barber's and tobacconist's, James Harwood's fine art dealer's and Thomas Marsden's clogger's in view. Note the crude clog-shaped signs outside Marsden's — glimpsed just above the hat of the liveried postillion on the left.

Ribchester hand-loom weavers — Mr James Watson and his family, pictured at their home, No.16 Church Street, *c.*1896.

The inauguration of the bore hole at Wycoller. Due to its growth, Colne found itself in need of more water and, in 1897, the Corporation originally planned a 120-million-gallon reservoir at Wycoller to alleviate the problem, but dropped the project on the grounds of cost. Instead, it looked for underground sources and drilling began in the summer of 1901, with water being struck at a depth of 420ft in September. The scheme was designed to supply the stream at Wycoller, with the water being extracted at Laneshawbridge and Bonny Booth for Colne's domestic supply. Among those on the picture are the first eight mayors of Colne.

22 June 1897 — 1,200ft up on the moors above the town, the Mayor of Darwen cuts the first sod for the erection of the landmark tower for which the townsfolk raised £4,000 in order to mark Queen Victoria's Diamond Jubilee. Earlier, a civic procession had taken place to Holy Trinity Church where, at a thanksgiving service, Darwen's growth from a village to a town of 38,000 people during the Queen's reign was recounted. Afterwards the local Rifle Volunteers fired a 'feu de joie' in the Market Place.

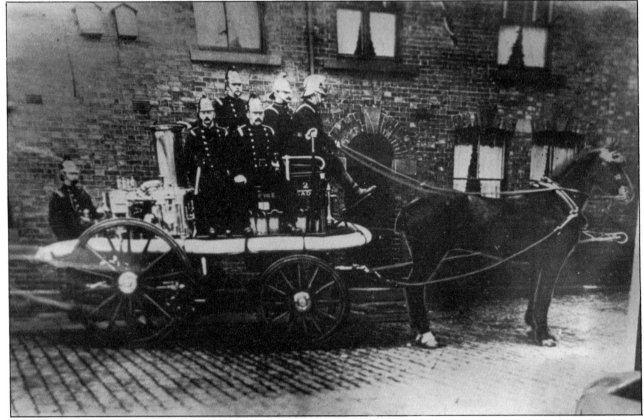

One of Blackburn's horse-drawn steam fire-engines outside the fire station in Clayton Street in 1905. A small fire brigade was in existence in the town in 1831 and appears to have possessed primitive manual engines for pumping water, according to a newspaper report of some being used to fight a fire at the Parish Church that year. A manual engine was bought by the recently-formed Corporation in 1856 and kept on the site of the present Town Hall. The town's force of firefighters was made up of lamplighters, watermen and journeymen employed by the Corporation who were summoned for emergency duties by the ringing of the market house bell. The Clayton Street fire station was built in 1867 and was used until the present-day fire station in Byrom Street opened in December 1921. In 1875, the town's first steam fire-engine was bought and the same year a volunteer fire brigade was formed as an auxiliary force. Up to acquiring its first motorised fire-engine in 1913, Blackburn had three steam engines and a stud of six horses, the last of which was kept until 1924.

The Loveclough works of the Rossendale Calico Printing Company were destroyed in a huge blaze in January 1906. The old *Northern Daily Telegraph* reported that 'notwithstanding the continued efforts of several brigades, the bigger portion of the extensive premises were gutted' and that the firm's 'large number of hands will be thrown out of employment for some time'.

A small fire, but big excitement for the onlookers. Only a few wooden sheds, containing oil and tubs, were destroyed when fire broke out in one of them at the pit bank at the Oswaldtwistle Colliery Company's Town Bent mine in March 1907. The Oswaldtwistle brigade, whose appliance is in the middle of the picture, prevented the fire from spreading, limiting the damage bill to £500.

21 June 1897 — a balloon ascent from Blackburn's market square to celebrate the Diamond Jubilee of Queen Victoria whose name is emblazoned on the massive sky ship. The huge crowd waited all day for the event billed for 7.30pm and it took one and a half hours for the balloon to be inflated with gas from a supply pipe, seen leading to it at the bottom left as it is weighted down with sandbags. The balloon belonged to Messrs Charles Spencer, Green and Sons, of London, and it was their aeronaut, Mr Spencer, and a passenger described as a 'Yorkshire gentleman' who made the flight. The balloon rose to 3,000 feet and came down 55 minutes later at West Bradford, near Clitheroe. In the background, at the right, is the Crown Hotel on Victoria Street which was extensively rebuilt after being ripped apart in a fatal gas explosion in 1891. It and the other buildings on Victoria Street were demolished in 1965.

Another angle on Blackburn's 1897 Royal Jubilee balloon ascent, as the long-awaited lift-off is about to happen. Behind the town's fish market, near the centre of the picture, is the Market Hall and clock tower. The building at the right housed T.and W.Thwaites' wines and spirit merchants.

June 1961 — ancient Towneley Hall provides a perfect period backdrop for the open-air production by local drama groups of *Merrie England,* one of the numerous events staged to mark the Centenary of the granting of Burnley's Royal charter of incorporation. This picture is of the dress rehearsal.

1904: 'Visiting Day at the Children's Fever Hospital,' says the original caption to this photograph. In the days before the discovery of antibiotics, when dreaded diseases like scarlet fever, diptheria and tuberculosis were potential killers, the closest that anxious parents got to their children being treated in the Blackburn Corporation Hospital for Infectious Diseases on visiting days was a glimpse of them through the windows — a system which prevailed until the 1950s. Built 600ft above sea level and 200ft above the town, in accordance with the belief that the supposedly-better air found at altitude was beneficial to tuberculosis cases, the hospital — present-day Park Lee — also set up a Residential Open-Air School in the grounds in 1923. Costing £20,000, the hospital opened in 1894 and had beds for 100 patients — adults as well as children.

Darwen's last bellman, Thomas T.Greenwood. Apart from being a human public-address system — announcing official proclamations, general tidings and matters of local interest — the bellman marched as a herald in mayoral processions and civic pageants. In the days of mail coaches, one the duties of Darwen's bellman was that of warning people to bring out their letters for despatching. Another less-official function was his role as a finder of lost children — going about with his bell to announce their disappearance. The town of Nelson maintained a bellman until 1899.

18 July 1912 — the unveiling in Limbrick, Blackburn, of the statue of 'Th' Owd Gam Cock', William Henry Hornby, the town's first mayor in 1851 and its MP for 12 years until 1869. The money for the £3,000 statue was left in 1907 in the will of Hornby's grateful employee, John Margerison, who worked for more than 50 years at Brookhouse Mills — Blackburn's first spinning mill, which Hornby's father had co-founded after moving to the town in 1779. The statue was unveiled by the baronet, Sir Harry Hornby, William Henry's son and MP for Blackburn for almost 24 years until 1910. A crowd of several thousand watched the ceemony, over which the Mayor, Alderman S.Crossley, presided.

Pleasington Hall, near Blackburn, was built in 1805-07 by John Francis Butler, whose father had bought the manor of Pleasington and the nearby Tudor mansion, Pleasington Old Hall, in 1780. But at the time this picture was taken, it was the home of Blackburn's MP, cotton manufacturer Sir Harry Hornby, who represented the town at Westminster from 1886 to 1910 without speaking once in the House of Commons. But after he and Lady Hornby left the house in 1914, after a 20-year tenancy, it fell into disrepair. It was demolished in 1932 after Blackburn Corporation bought the hall and 100 surrounding acres for the creation of Pleasington Cemetery. Note the lawnmower in this picture, being pulled by a donkey.

Upstairs, downstairs. The staff of Pleasington Hall, near Blackburn, in the early 1900s. Sir Harry and Lady Hornby had 17 servants to look after them.

Special trains were put on by the Lancashire and Yorkshire Railway Company on the line between Blackburn and Pleasington and to Cherry Tree for this event at Pleasington Hall in September 1906. And the trams from town were also packed. The occasion was a Conservative Party fete, hosted at their home by Blackburn MP Sir Harry Hornby and his wife. More than 7,000 people attended — 'a large proportion being ladies' — and, as well as enjoying games like egg-and-spoon races and refreshments served in two large marquees, the guests were entertained with music by the Blackburn Town Band, the Police and Fire Brigade Band and St Stephen's Fife and Drum Band. Lady Hornby is pictured standing at the centre, with a woman in a period invalid carriage.

The Hornby statue in Limbrick, Blackburn — looking across Sudell Cross down Northgate, with the Sessions House and Public Halls in the centre of the picture. The 10ft 9in hollow bronze statue on its 13ft 6in grey granite pedestal was moved in 1968 when it became an obstruction to traffic. It was re-sited alongside the Town Hall in King William Street in 1970, being unveiled by its subject's 81-year-old grandson, Sir Russell Hornby.

Good Friday was the occasion for a day in the country for many East Lancashire working folk. Here, in the Edwardian era, hundreds of Burnley people have ventured only as far as the stepping-stones over the River Calder at Ightenhill. The stones were later replaced by a footbridge.

Fine weather on Good Fridays also brought crowds to the banks of the River Ribble at Brungerley Bridge, Clitheroe. Nearby Brungerley Park opened in 1876 while downstream, boating and swinging-boat amusement rides were also big attractions.

May 1878 — Clayton Grange, at Clayton-le-Dale, near Blackburn, reduced to a burned-out shell by rioting cotton workers. The house was the home of Colonel Robert Raynsford Jackson, chairman of the textile employers' federation. His home took the brunt of the mob's fury after the bosses met to reduce workers' wages by 10 per cent because of bad trade. Before venting their anger there, the rioters, fired up at a 5,000-strong meeting at Blakey Moor in Blackburn, had smashed windows in several of the town's mills. The colonel and his family managed to escape in a brougham before the mob arrived to do £12,000-worth of damage at his home. All that survived was a barometer. The rioters even burned a four-wheeled carriage in the coach house and dragged its remains in triumph to Blackburn where it was finally flung into the river at Ewood. The Riot Act was read and troops were called out from Preston, but a second day of rioting ensued, with 64 houses in Preston New Road having their windows broken. The ring-leader, a man called Smalley, was later sentenced to 15 years' penal servitude and eight other prisoners were jailed for periods ranging from 15 years to 12 months. Clayton Grange was rebuilt, but demolished in 1955. Its destruction in 1878 is still recalled in souvenir pottery produced at the time.

Now a ruin, Woodfold Hall at Mellor was built in 1798 by cotton magnate Henry Sudell, then the largest employer of home-based hand-loom weavers in Blackburn. His wealth and influence were such that when, in 1818, 6,000 weavers marched on the mansion to demand better wages, he agreed to a five per cent increase, knowing that other employers would have to follow suit. The bells of Blackburn's Parish Church were rung to greet the deal. Reputed to be a millionaire by the time he was 56 in 1820, Sudell was bankrupt seven years later — the consequence of a failed foreign specualtion. He left Blackburn for Wiltshire and died in Bath, aged 92. In 1877, the house, built from stone quarried at Abbott Brow, Mellor, was bought by Blackburn brewer and MP, Daniel Thwaites. The house was lived in by his daughter, Mrs Elma Yerburgh, who moved to Scotland at the outbreak of World War Two and lent the hall to elderly women evacuees from Liverpool. Becoming too expensive to run or sell in the period of post-war austerity, the house was emptied in 1949 and left to decay.

The interior of Woodfold Hall, Mellor, before World War Two when it was occupied by Mrs Elma Yerburgh, one of Blackburn's most prominent citizens, noted charity worker and the town's first woman Freeman. Despite its opulence, the house had no electricity.

21 June 1882 — schoolchildren line up on Darwen's new market place for the opening of the town's Market Hall. The building, which, together with the site, cost £31,000, was opened with a golden key by the MP, Mr F.W.Grafton. After speeches from the balcony, the celebrations continued with a public banquet in the Co-operative Hall and a ball in the Market Hall. Previously, the site had housed some old saw mills, a bleach works nearly a century old, cottages and a lodge full of dirty water.

Blackburn police mounted section, pictured outside the Fire Police Station in Clayton Street in 1897 during the celebrations for Queen Victoria's Diamond Jubilee. The town's fire-brigade and police were merged in 1882 and a mounted police section formed ten years later, consisting of eight constables and one acting sergeant — all, apart from two, former cavalry soldiers. In the centre of the picture, on a fire-brigade horse borrowed for the occasion, is Isaac Lewis, Chief Constable of Blackburn from 1887 to 1913. The Borough Police abandoned the use of horses in 1933 and the town's force, formed with the creation of the Corporation in 1851, was merged with Lancashire Constabulary in 1969.

Clayton-le-Moors fire brigade — a picture taken before World War One when the town's fire crew also included a bugler. The team's driver was known as 'Long Tom'.

Elizabeth Ann Lewis — 'The Drunkard's Friend'. One hymn, sung by the inebriates she saved, began: "When ev'ry drunkard in Blackburn has been saved from the drink and in Lees Hall is seen standing beside Blackburn's Teetotal Queen, that will be glory for you and me."

1924 — the funeral of Blackburn's 'Temperance Queen,' Mrs Elizabeth Ann Lewis. Also known as the 'Drunkard's Friend', Mrs Lewis waged a life-long battle against drink, starting in 1882 when the town had 604 licensed premises and the reputation of being the 'most beery town in England'. Waging her campaign at the Lees Hall Mission in Mincing Lane — now the headquarters of the town's St John Ambulance — and at outdoor meetings, she persuaded thousands to sign the pledge and became the object of a virtual personality cult, having anthems dedicated to her and her movement. When she died, thousands filed past her coffin as she lay 'in state' for two days in the Lees Hall and the two-mile route of her funeral procession to Blackburn Cemetery was lined by townsfolk. Out of respect, her adversaries, the publicans, closed their doors for the occasion. The teetotal mission she founded finally closed in 1973.

Stanhill Village, near Oswaldtwistle, lays claim to being one the birthplaces of the Industrial Revolution. It was here, in 1764, that James Hargreaves — or Hargraves — invented the spinning jenny that increased and speeded up the production of yarn for the weaving industry and helped to lead to the introduction of the factory system for mass production. A memorial garden in his honour was created alongside his former home at Stanhill in 1957, but at the time of his invention, he became hated by local hand spinners who feared his multi-spindle jenny would deprive them of their livelihoods. In the face of their persecution, the inventor moved to Nottingham where he died in 1778.

1 September 1923 — the Chief Scout, Sir Robert (later, Lord) Baden-Powell, at the centre of the picture, reviews 5,000 Scouts, Guides and Wolf Cubs at a Lancashire rally at Witton Park, Blackburn. 'St George' in shining armour (left), was part of a 'dream story', enacted for the 7,000 spectators. In it, a 'ragged urchin,' played by a member of the Blackburn Grammar School troop, encountered the saintly warrior and was asked if he would like to enter a better land. On agreeing, he was told that first he must become a Scout — upon which his rags fell away to reveal the sort of uniformed, clean-living, unselfish youngster that Baden-Powell's movement idealised. Here, the Boer War hero Chief Scout, accompanied on the platform by Assistant County Commissioner G.W.Besley, has a trilby-hatted Press corps in close attendance.

Sausage, peas and new potatoes, served up with light classical music played by the Liverpool Philharmonic Orchestra, were on the menu in the works canteen for 3,000 employees at the Mullard electronics factory in Blackburn in July 1955. Conductor Hugo Rignold, however, got a large fruit cake in the shape of a music book, iced with the score of Handel's 'Largo' — a gift of the canteen staff. The occasion was the orchestra's first experiment in 'industrial concerts' since the wartime days of 'Music While You Work'.

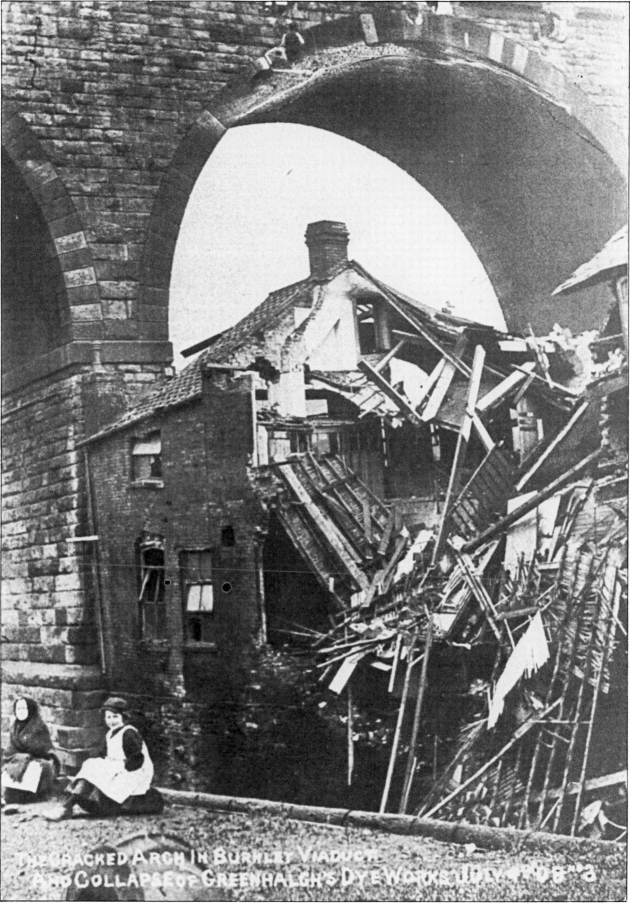

The old-time photographer got the date wrong when he penned his caption on to the negative of this picture. The date was 9 July 1908 — not the 4th, as he wrote — when a large part of Greenhalgh's dyeworks in the Calder Vale area of Burnley collapsed. The firm had, in fact, had warning of the event the previous day — when it was found that doors inside the building would not close and windows began to crack while land in the area also began cracking up. Then, at 5.30am the next day, residents in the vicinity heard a noise like thunder and found the dyeworks, on the banks of the River Brun, in ruins. The subsidence in the area was blamed on quicksands that were found to be 12ft deep. The collapse of the works was followed by the cracking of the nearby railway viaduct and pieces of masonry falling off. Train services were suspended and fearful residents evacuated to temporary sleeping quarters in the nearby paper works. The damage cost the dyeworks, uninsured against subsidence, was some £3,000.

THE DAMAGED ARCH BURNLEY.

Repairing the subsidence-damaged railway viaduct at Calder Vale, Burnley, in 1908, meant first shoring it up with huge baulks of timber and removing masonry loosened by the cracks in the structure. Barricades had to be erected to keep curious crowds at a safe distance. Two hundred workmen were employed on the repair work for weeks.

In 1954, 13-year-old Bobby was facing redundancy as the last horse left at Blackburn's railway station where he had worked for eight years — on shunting duties and, previously, on delivery runs. Forty years before, the station had 180 working horses. Bobby, who cost £1.25 a day to feed, is pictured with shunt horse driver Bob Walker.

Sunday School children process through Oswaldtwistle on 22 June 1911, as the town celebrates the Coronation of King George V. Clubs, friendly societies, the civic authorities and tradesmen's turn-outs also joined the march to and from Rhyddings Park where a loyal resolution was passed. In the background (left) is the tower of Holy Trinity Church which was consecrated in 1888.

'Walking Day' for schoolchildren in Sabden in 1905. The village's school, founded in 1837 by politician and free trade advocate Richard Cobden, was one of the first in the country to be opened free of any denominational link.

Church Street, Padiham, is thronged with walkers and watchers in this pre-World War One view of the annual Whit Monday procession, with the Parish Church, St Leonard's, at the right. The town's church processions are now held on Trinity Sunday.

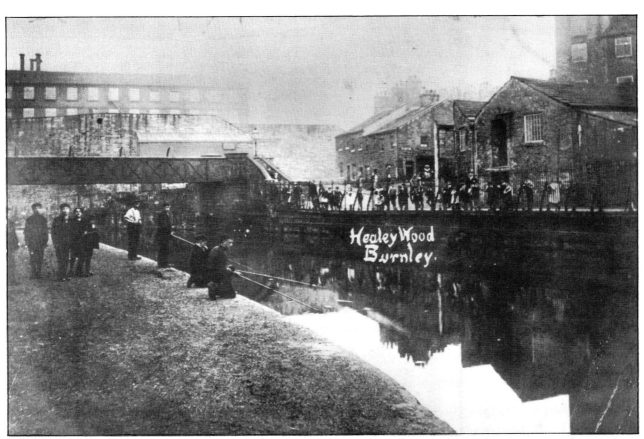

Fishing on the Leeds-Liverpool canal at Healey Wood, Burnley. The footbridge over the 'cut' linked Healey Wood Road with Cooper Street.

A cavalier theme was the topic of this carnival float, pictured in Dandy Walk, Blackburn, early this century.

1953 — Blackburn's celebrations for the Coronation of Queen Elizabeth II included a giant procession of churches through the town centre. Here, youngsters from the Church of the Saviour cross Salford. In the background (right) is the Cinema Royal in Ainsworth Street.

May Day, 1907 — an unknown Blackburn group. This picture shows the long-gone children's tradition of dressing up and dancing around a home-made maypole on 1 May. Groups of such children went from street to street, hoping to earn coppers with their routine. The girls used to sing: "Round and round the maypole, merrily we go. Tripping, tripping, lightly singing as we go. All the happy pastimes are on the village green. A-dancing in the sunshine, hurrah for May Queen." Sometimes, however, the second line was altered to: "Treading like an elephant, groaning as we go." These May Day girls' groups were often accompanied by a 'bear' — a boy covered by a hessian sack with its corners tied to resemble the animal's ears and mimicking the real dancing bears that were brought to the streets by itinerant showmen. The May Day 'bear' would go through a routine of acrobatics while the girls would chant the 'Adi-on-con-kay' song that the handlers of the real bears used.

Blackburn Borough Reference Library, 1926 — part of the town's Museum since 1975 following the Library's transfer to county council control and its move to the old Co-operative Society emporium in nearby Town Hall Street.

The giant Calderstones mental hospital, near Whalley, was nearing completion at the end of 1914 when the horrific level of World War One casualties on the Western Front led to it being pressed into service as the 2,110-bed Queen Mary's Military Hospital. More than 57,000 wounded British and Allied troops were treated there before the hospital eventually took on its intended role in 1922. A special railway halt was built in the grounds. It could take as little as 24 hours for soldiers to be transported from the battlefield across the Channel to ports like Southampton and on by rail to Calderstones. Many arrived still with the mud of the trenches on their uniforms. Wards at the hospital were named alphabetically, with 'L' being omitted because of its grim phonetic association with 'hell'. Here, bedfast convalescents wait for the cinema show, staged on Saturdays, by the hospital's entertainment committee.

Skating on Queen's Park lake, Blackburn, in January 1946. Fourteen degrees of frost put 2.5 inches of ice on the lake's surface early that month — and such a huge strain on gas supplies that consumers were urged to economise.

The Britannia Inn, Penny Street, Blackburn, decorated for the Coronation of King George V in 1911. In the doorway stands licensee James Barlow and his wife, Maggie. Next door to the left is the shop of watch and clockmakers W.H.Tomlinson & Son and, far left, the premises of window ticket and show card writers W.V.Rice & Sons — a business which expired in 1976 after 94 years in Blackburn. At the time, the other pubs in Penny Street were the Welcome, the Shamrock, the Pheasant, the Plough, the Ship, the Fleece and the Waterloo Hotel.

The size of the Bull's Head Hotel in Whalley New Road, Blackburn, near the Wilpshire boundary, testified to the wealth of the brewing industry when it was built in 1907. It had room for two billiard tables and, despite the advent of the motoring era, large stables at the rear which later became home for Wilpshire Riding School.

The Sportsman's Arms at the corner of Shear Brow and Pleckgate Road, Blackburn, looks slightly different today from this view, taken soon after World War One — a gable was added at roof level and later removed. Then, as well as billiards, it offered a two-stall stable to let. Licensee James Thompson Kay is pictured at the doorway with his daughter, Alice, and son, Richard, each wearing shiny clogs.

1953 — Finishing touches are put to the Coronation decorations at the entrance to Hindley Brothers' Bankfield Mills at Nelson.

The Mayor of Burnley's Civic Sunday procession of 1954 included the first appearance of dogs among the contingent. Trained to locate victims by scent in rescue operations, they belonged to the town's Civil Defence corps.

Once a common sight in East Lancashire's streets — swilling and mopping the pavement flags outside the front door. The houseproud also embellished their doorsteps and window ledges with white and cream markings from 'donkey' stones which they often obtained in exchange from rag and bone men.

Getting away from it all. Queues of holidaymakers on Burnley's Cattle Market get ready to depart by bus for the seaside at the start of the town's 'Fair' week in 1930. As well as clothes, the vacationers' suitcases often contained food which the landladies of their resort boarding houses would cook for them during their stay.

The speed of this charabanc was 12 mph — which must have meant long hours on the road for this 1927 outing to Scarborough by workers from the Blackburn textile accessories firm of Jones Textilaties.

Burnley's annual fair — seen here on a thronged Cattle Market during the town's 1922 holiday week — traces its history back to the charter granted in 1294 by Edward I for the town's market and a fair lasting three days. First held around the Market Cross near St Peter's Church, the original fairs were mainly for the sale of goods and animals, but also included entertainment by minstrels, morris-dancers, jugglers and acrobats. Shortly after 1800, the market and fair was moved to the junction of Market Street (now Manchester Road) and St James' Street. In 1865, the Corporation bought the land in Parker Lane which became the Cattle Market where the fair, increasingly given over to amusement rides and booths, was held until 1949. Here, among the attractions is the booth (right) of gypsy crystal gazer Madame Rachel while, nearer the centre of the picture, is a stall where patrons could have their weight and height measured for a penny. This view was probably taken from the upstairs of the now-vanished Rose and Thistle pub in Parker Lane.

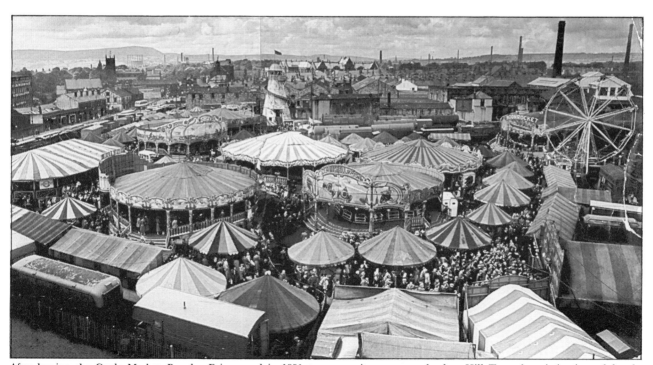

After leaving the Cattle Market, Burnley Fair moved in 1951 to a new site on vacant land at Hill Top where it is pictured for the first time in this view. In the distance, behind Church Street at the left of the picture, is St Peter's Church — the spot near where the fair had begun more than 650 years earlier. In 1956, the fair was transferred to its present site on Fulledge Recreation Ground. This view of the site alongside Dixon's boiler works — a spot now occupied by Sainsbury's supermarket — was taken from the top of the now-vanished Odeon Cinema.

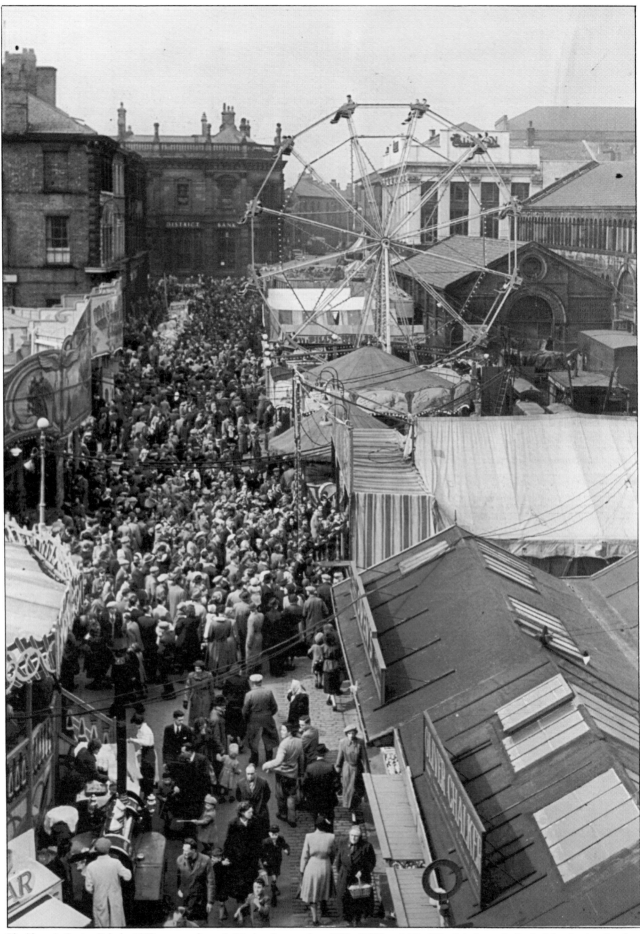

Blackburn's Easter Fair in 1952 — crowds pack Market Street where Billy Williams' Big Wheel is located, flanked by the booths that specialised in freak shows such as the Fat Man and Lady, the Flea Circus and animals with five legs. The fair was first held on Blackburn's market place and by the Market House in 1852, although the town had an Easter Fair in 1750 and a May Day Fair long before that. Note the hot potato cart at the bottom left.

Easter Fair amusement rides on Blackburn's market place in the 1930s. In 1891 and 1892, the Corporation banned it from this spot and the event was held on the parade ground of Canterbury Street Barracks and the nearby Wrangling. The fair was last held on the Market Place in 1964 prior to redevelopment of the site of the town's main shopping precinct. Since then, it has been located at Birley Street, Ewood, Barton Street and, more recently, at Witton Park.

June 1945 — with victory won in Europe, Britain's wartime leader, Winston Churchill (right), took to the election trail, calling at Turf Moor, Burnley, to spell out the Conservatives' message and speak in support of the Tory-backed National Liberal candidate for Burnley, Major H.H.M.Milnes. Together they toured the town centre in a Humber convertible before arriving at the football ground where a crowd of 10,000 waited. It was wasted journey — at the polls, Major Milne lost by more than 13,000 to the Socialist candidate, Mr W.A.Burke, and Churchill was swept from power in the Labour landslide victory.

22 February 1939 — Blackburn's Public Halls are packed as they have never been before as 14,000 people, paying sixpence to half a crown, hear Britain's political hero of the hour, Prime Minister Neville Chamberlain. King George's Hall is filled to capacity and so, too, are the Assembly Hall and Lecture Theatre below where the audiences listen to the Premier's hour-long speech by relay. Even greater crowds are outside the building. The message is 'Peace for our time' — following the deal which Chamberlain thought he had struck with the German dictator, Adolf Hitler, during the Munich crisis five months earlier. But within days of his triumphant hour at Blackburn, Chamberlain is to see that Hitler is not appeased as Nazi troops occupy what is left of Czechoslovakia and he makes Poland the next target of his territorial ambitions — a step that, within six months of the celebration of the paper peace at Blackburn, will plunge Britain into war.

Standing at the centre of the stage of King George's Hall, Blackburn, in February 1939, Prime Minister Neville Chamberlain gives a peace message to a rapt audience and (left) to the representatives of the world's Press.

9 February 1963 — with his trademarks of a Gannex raincoat and pipe, Harold Wilson (centre), is on the brink of becoming leader of the Labour Party as he walks through Blackburn's outdoor market with the town's MP, Barbara Castle, accompanied by former local party chairman Harry Eastwood, on their way to a regional conference. The following year, the parliamentary pair were Cabinet colleagues.

His real name was Robert Reynolds, but to a generation of Blackburn folk before World War One, he was better known as 'Owd Chipper' — the rag and bone man with a portable peep show. Born in 1824, he was said to be fascinated as a youngster by the world of the theatre and, despite parental disapproval, appeared at the old Theatre Royal as an extra in a play called 'A Chip Off The Old Block' — from which he acquired his nickname. A spinner by trade, he turned showman in his own right by mounting on a handcart a peep show — made up of old war pictures and some toy soldiers to depict such events as Napoleon's battles and the Boer War battle of Spion Kop. The 'admission fee' to Owd Chipper's show was a handful of rags or a few empty bottles, but thousands of children happily paid up. The story goes that any child who asked which of the candlelit figures in the peep show was Napoleon would be told: "Any on 'em!" Reynolds died in 1912.

James Whittaker — alias 'Jimmy Pudding' — was a character who literally left his mark on Burnley around the turn of the century. Born in Colne, he worked for many Burnley butchers and got his nickname from his association with the black pudding firm of Slater's, whose premises were on St James' Street, next door to the White Lion pub. He gained renown, however, after serving several years in prison for a crime he claimed he did not commit, but of which he had been convicted on evidence hinging on his footprints. He vowed never to be caught by the same trap again and, for the rest of his days, he went around with thick lumps of leather nailed to the soles of his clogs in order to make his footprints unique. Jimmy spent the last four years of his life in the workhouse, but, on his death at the age of 78 in 1917, the *Burnley News* said of him: "He was too proud to beg, too honest to steal."

Fred Kempster, 8ft 4in tall and weighing 27st, was known as the Blackburn Giant. But his association with the town stems mainly from his ill luck in dying there, aged 29, in April 1918. Hailing from the Wiltshire village of Avebury, Fred went on tour as a young man, signed up by a showman who billed him as 'The World's Tallest Man'. He was in Germany when World War One broke out and was interned until the US ambassador secured his release in 1916. He was on display in Cohen's Penny Bazaar in Victoria Street, Blackburn, when he took ill in 1918 and it took eight men to carry him into an ambulance on a fire-brigade jumping sheet. And he was so tall that he could not be carried up the staircase at the town's Queen's Park Hospital, so he had to be admitted by the fire escape instead. A large crowd witnessed his funeral and he was buried in two graves, dug end-to-end, at Blackburn Cemetery — it taking 14 men to lower his 9ft-long coffin into the grave. Here, Fred is pictured with his mother. One of his tricks was to remove a ring from his finger and pass an old penny through it.

 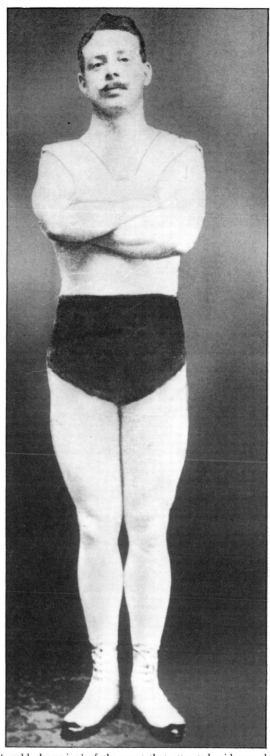

The jumping feats of Blackburn's Jack Higgins are legendary. He was the 'world champion' of the sport that attracted widespread working-class interest and bets up and down the country. Born in the King Street area of town, he literally leapt to fame in the 1890s with the soaring stunts that he turned into a career. At 18, at the town's Ohmy's Circus, he jumped over the heads of 20 horses and in and out of seven wash tubs, each spaced three yards apart. He could also clear the canal — and touch the surface with one foot in mid-flight. Another of his tricks was jumping into a crate of eggs and out again without cracking a single shell. At the age of 55, in 1927, he jumped over a horse and cab at the New Princes Theatre in Blackburn. Jack took his gravity-defying act countrywide and on a 25,000-mile tour of America, taking on all-comers. But as well as using muscle-power, he and fellow jumpers also gained extra impetus from the hand-weights they used, swinging them backwards and swiftly discarding them in order to gain an extra boost for their leaps. Jack found fame which still lasts today, but not a fortune. He was almost penniless when he died in the late 1940s.

Diminutive Richard Thompson performed for coppers on Blackburn's market place and any other place a crowd might gather. His prowess at lifting heavy weights and escapology earned him the nickname, 'Strong Dick'. But he is best remembered for a famous feat that never came off — his 'Walk to China' in the early 1890s. The event caught the town's imagination and he was given a rousing send-off, but on reaching Darwen Moors just a few miles into the journey, he stopped a farmer and asked him: "Can tha tell me which is t' way to China?" The puzzled farmer said he had no idea, prompting Dick to abandon the hike. The beefy bantam died in 1945, aged 77. But even today those asking a Blackburnian to do an over-arduous job stand to get the reply: "Who do you think I am — Strong Dick?"

30 September 1905 — 200,000 people lined Blackburn's streets and packed the Boulevard for the arrival of Princess Louise, Duchess of Argyll, on the occasion of her unveiling the statue the town had erected to her mother, Queen Victoria, after her death in 1901. The public appeal fund for the project in fact raised too much, with the surplus of more than £55 being divided between the Royal Infirmary and the District Nurses' Home. The 11ft-high statue of white Sicilian marble, erected on a 14ft grey granite pedestal, cost £2,500 and almost another £1,000 was spent on the surrounds built on the site given by the Parish Church. The sculptor was Australian-born Bertram Mackennal, who had gained recognition as a protegé of the world-famous singer, Nellie Melba.

7 July 1936 — Great Harwood's first royal visitor, the Duke of Kent, walks down a flag-decked Queen Street, with council chairman, Mrs G.M.Boardman on his right. Earlier, the Duke had visited the Social Service Men's Occupational Centre in Town Hall Street where unemployed workers were instructed in such crafts as cobbling and carpentry. Then, he walked the 300 yards to the Mercer Hall where classes for jobless women workers were held.

July 1913 — a royal motorcade passes along the Boulevard as King George V and Queen Mary make Blackburn their calling point during their week-long visit to Lancashire that took in more than 30 towns as well as the cities of Manchester and Liverpool. Earlier, they had visited Roe Lee Mill at Blackburn and called at the Town Hall where the King laid the foundation stone to the new public halls — by remote control. On the platform outside the Town Hall, he pressed a button which sent a signal to a crane at the Northgate site and the stone was lowered into place. Among the cars in this picture are three being used by the Press corps.

After visiting Blackburn on their royal tour of Lancashire in 1913, King George V and Queen Mary called at Darwen where they were greeted on a garlanded platform outside the town's civic buildings. Seen near the centre of the picture, the royal couple are about to depart on another leg of their week-long, 300-mile tour of the county.

May 1888 — the Prince and Princess of Wales, later Edward VII and Queen Alexandra, depart from Blackburn after laying the foundation stone of the town's new Technical School in Blakey Moor. Heading for the railway station, the King can be seen doffing his hat in the royal carriage to acknowledge the cheers of the crowd which fills Railway Road and the Boulevard and, at the far right, had even taken to the rooftops as well as the windows. To the left of the Adelphi Hotel is a billboard site behind which the *Northern Daily Telegraph's* new offices would open in 1894. Meantime, the 18-month old newspaper is located in its first offices further down Railway Road, glimpsed in the centre of this picture where its signboard protrudes at second-floor level. At the right is a guard of honour formed by the 2nd Lancashire Rifle Volunteers while following the royal car is an escort of men of the 9th Lancers.

Work

The canalside wharf of Blackburn coal merchants Crook & Thompson in 1920. The company's origins could then be traced back 110 years to before the canal was completed through Blackburn in 1816. John Thompson, of Hoghton, brought coal from Wigan by barge to the then-terminus at Riley Green of the canal's western length and carted it to customers in the Blackburn and Preston area. But with the coming of the railway to Blackburn in 1846, the company set up a depot at Whalley Banks and later also had three wharves in the town. This one was at Audley Bridge. In 1877, when the firm became Crook & Thompson, it had only three delivery horses, but, by 1920, the number was 36. The truck being used by the young boy is marked with the company's white-bordered black diamond symbol which also appeared on its barges. Anyone buying a hundredweight of coal was allowed to borrow the truck to take its contents home.

Town Bent Colliery was one of the 15 coal mines operating in the Oswaldtwistle and Church area in the nineteenth century and, at its peak, the East Lancashire coalfield, centred on Burnley, Accrington and Rossendale, had some 50 pits. Coal mining was second only to textiles as the major employer. At the turn of the century, Oswaldtwistle's three major mines, Aspen, Lower Darwen and Town Bent employed some 1,000 men and boys. Town Bent closed in 1925 as its seams were worked out.

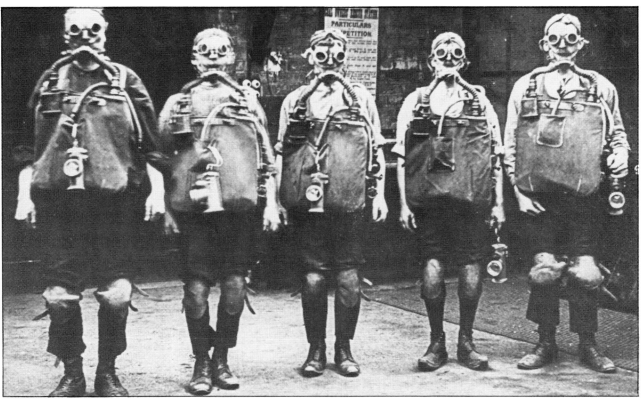

Members of the rescue team at Town Bent Colliery, Oswaldtwistle. Note their primitive headwear, breathing appartus, lamps and knee pads. According to the notice in the background, they seem to be taking part in a competition staged by the coal owners' association.

Martholme Colliery, near Great Harwood, before World War One. Some of the workers gathered here on the pithead are mere boys.

Bank Hall Colliery, Burnley, in 1954. Sunk in 1860, it was the town's biggest pit, with a 1,500ft-deep main shaft. It also had the longest tunnel in the coalfield — at more than six miles long, it stretched nearly to Colne and it took men 45 minutes to reach the coalface. At its peak, Bank Hall employed 1,000 men and when it was closed in 1971 for safety reasons — too much gas — its 725 workers had produced 330,000 tons of coal a year. The site has now been transformed into 50 acres of parkland.

March 1942 — miners ascending from the night shift at Calder Pit, Simonstone, which closed 16 years later when its reserves were exhausted. The man wearing a helmet is a shot-firer — identified by the padlocked explosives bag on his belt.

The Coke Works at Altham in 1960, then in the ownership of the National Coal Board. Here, until 1949, also stood Moorfield Colliery. Two and a half years after it opened, the pit was the scene in 1883 of East Lancashire's worst mining disaster, with 68 workers — some of them boys as young as ten — killed in a colossal underground explosion. An estimated crowd of 20,000 people gathered at the pithead on hearing news of the catastrophe.

Seen from the air in the 1940s, the Moorfield Colliery and Chemical Works at Altham was then in the ownership of the Lancashire Foundry Coke Company whose giant ovens were used to supply gas and other by-products. Among those who worked there as a 'Bevin Boy' during the World War Two was comedian Eric Morecambe.

The weaving shed at Hole House Mill, Blackburn, c.1911. At this time, out of the town's population of 133,000, almost 42,000 were working in textiles. And, with more than 28,300 of them tending looms like these, Blackburn employed more weavers than any other town in the world. Burnley was close behind, with nearly 26,000 weavers. The years before World War One were generally a boom time for the cotton industry. Between 1910 and 1911, the number of looms in Blackburn soared by over 19,500 to 87,377. And from the start of the century to the outbreak of the war, 21 new mills were built in the town, bringing its total to 150. As the young faces in this picture show, many of the mill workers were children. Out of Blackburn's massive weaving workforce in 1911, 814 were boys and girls as young as 12, working on the half-time system which required them to also spend half a day at school. The half-time system ended in 1920. Hole House Mill's weaving shed contained some 800 looms about the time this picture was taken. It ceased weaving in 1959.

Power loom overlookers, like these pictured with the manager at Roe Lee Mill, Blackburn, were known familiarly as 'tacklers'. They mended and maintained the looms and weavers, who earned only piece rates, depended on their skill to keep their machines and income from coming to a halt. They were noted for their caprice and supposed gaumlessness which made them the subject of many ''Tacklers' Tales'' jokes.

The drawing-in room at Moscow Mill, off Union Road, Oswaldtwistle, about 1900. The drawer's apprentice was known as a 'reacher' and his mistakes often earned him a sharp kick on the shins from his superior's clogs.

Shuttle-making at the Addison Street works in Blackburn of Rowland Baguley and Company, *c.*1920. The company began in Manchester in 1840, but moved to Blackburn in 1854 where it took over part of the Eagle Foundry in Starkie Street. The firm bought and converted the old Gas Street Mill in 1878, extending it in 1881 and 1889. Some 50 employees produced a wide range of shuttles for the home textile industry and for export before it closed in the early 1930s.

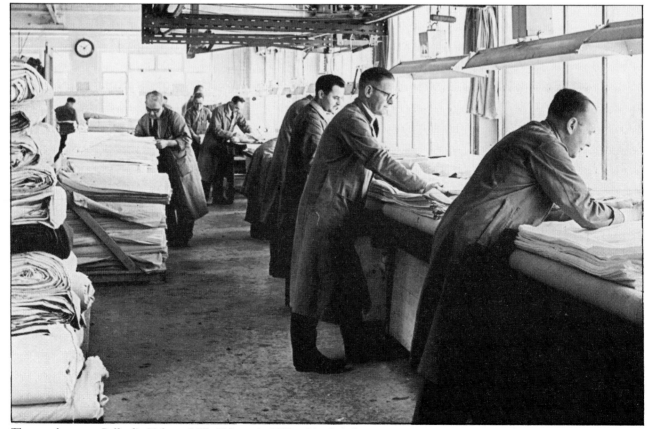

The warehouse at Pollard's Malvern Mill, Nelson, in 1955, with cloth inspectors at work. Often known as 'cut lookers' — because they looked for faults in the lengths of finished cloth that weavers had cut from their looms — they also calculated how much was woven, so that the piece-work weavers' wages could be calculated.

The engine house at George Whiteley's Albion Mill, Livesey, in 1951. The spinning and weaving mill, built in 1856-58, came to a halt in 1975 due to a shortage of orders. But in 1951, when this picture was taken, it was its double-beam steam engine that was at the end of the road as the mill converted to electricity to drive its machines. The 50-ton flywheel, seen here, turned at 18,630 revolutions per day. It was broken up for scrap.

Loom-making at the British Northrop Loom Company in Blackburn in the 1940s. In its hey-day the firm employed 2,700 workers, producing 10,000 automatic looms a year on a massive site in the Little Harwood district. It was established in 1902 by William Livesey of Greenbank Iron Works and others to import the automatic loom invented in the USA in the previous decade. By 1905, the loom was being made at the Greenbank works, with the first Northrop building being erected in 1907 and the company's payroll growing to 220 by 1914. Decline began in the late 1950s and, by 1968, the workforce had dropped below 500. Demolition and a massive fire in 1982 in a large part of the works which was used for storage mean that only one building of the formerly-immense Northrop works remains today, being used as an industrial and commercial complex.

Globe Works, Accrington, in the 1960s. The textile machinery firm of Howard and Bullough — specialising in spinning equipment — built a market in 43 countries throughout the world in the century following its formation in 1853 by James Bullough. At its peak, the factory employed 8,000 — on war work. Even after the decline in the textile industry in the 1950s, the firm was still employing 3,500 in the 1960s, but was involved in mergers and shrinkage during the following two decades. Now, after a management buy-out, the business' payroll is down to 70 and departure from the huge Globe Works scheduled.

The yard of cart and coachbuilders and blacksmiths J.& S.Leaver at Eanam, Blackburn. The firm, which started in a tiny cottage nearby in 1844, was among the first in the town to enter the car business and, in 1917, became Blackburn's first Austin dealership. It continues today at Eanam as part of the Manchester-based Lookers car retailing group.

Transport

Bank Hall Colliery, Burnley, 1954 — canal barges belonging to Blackburn coal merchants Crook & Thompson being loaded.

The Leeds-Liverpool canal at Blackburn in 1960, with now-vanished Whitebirk power station in the background. The electricity plant, opened by Blackburn Corporation as the Blackburn (East) Generating Station in 1921, originally had wooden cooling towers. Its four, 250ft reinforced concrete towers were erected between 1942 and 1954. The power station consumed vast tonnages of coal brought by canal from the Burnley coalfield. But the waterway was doomed as a commercial artery by the 13-week 'Big Freeze' winter of early 1963 which kept the canal ice-bound for so long that the transport of freight by barge in East Lancashire never recovered. Generating ended at Whitebirk in 1976, although the cooling towers were not demolished until 1983.

1954 — launch of a 60ft barge after a re-fit at the boat builder's yard of T. & J.Hodson, founded at Whitebirk, Blackburn, in 1870. All the timber used in the construction of the barge was of English oak, except for the deck which was made of pitchpine.

The entrance to the Mile Tunnel — actually 1,630 yards long — on the canal at Foulridge. Opened in 1796, the tunnel took five years to construct. Moored at the right is the old steam tug, *Foulridge*, which was employed to tow horse-drawn boats through the tunnel — sometimes more than a dozen at a time. The boat had a rudder fore and aft so that it did not need to turn around and was fitted with breathing apparatus to prevent its pilot from being overcome by fumes from the boiler. The tug was withdrawn from regular service in 1937, having been made increasingly redundant by the introduction of self-powered barges.

Buttercup, the cow, made it all the way through the canal's Mile Tunnel at Foulridge under her own steam in September 1912. Owned by Robin Brown, of Blue Slate Farm, Colne, she plunged into the cut at the Barrowford end of the tunnel and, unable to get out, swam its entire length to Foulridge where she was pulled out — and, according to local legend, revived with the better part of a bottle of brandy.

The Manchester Road wharf on the Leeds-Liverpool canal at Burnley when it was an important and busy distribution point for the town's industries. Now, the place is a tourist attraction.

This curious-looking steam railmotor took to the rails in 1905 — in competition with the electric tram. The Lancashire and Yorkshire railway introduced it on Bury-Holcombe Brook line after losing passengers to the tramway between Bury and Tottington which had been electrified the previous year. The railmotor was equipped with retractable steps so that extra halts could be created at places which had no raised platforms. It also ran later between Burnley and Colne before being replaced by a new design in 1909.

This 1930s train was carrying a cargo of Nelson's most famous confection, the Victory V lozenge. Millions of the tongue-warming sweet were made each week at the firm's six-acre factory and were exported all over the world. The business began in 1830 when local man Thomas Fryer met a travelling confectioner and the pair opened a shop and eventually a factory, but the famous lozenge was invented by Dr Edward Smith who bought the firm in 1850. An EC ban on one of Victory V's ingredients, chloroform, took the bite out of sales in the 1980s and the Nelson factory — famous also for its jelly babies — closed in 1987.

James Retford, the bearded man on the left, was in charge of the engine, *Mazeppa*, and was Burnley's most famous driver of his day. He took the train which ran between Burnley and Todmorden in the 1850s and '60s. Then, six trains a day ran to Todmorden between 7.30am and 5.30pm, with the same number of return journeys.

The end of the line for steam — the scene at the marshalling yards at Rose Grove, Burnley, in 1968 as redundant Stanier 8F locos
wait to make their last journey to the scrapyard.

Wilpshire Station, the second halt out of Blackburn on the Hellifield line, was originally named Ribchester — being intended not
only to serve Wilpshire, but also the Ribble Valley village some four miles distant from the track. The station, which also had a freight
yard, closed in 1964, two years after the Beeching axe removed passenger services from the line.

Rose Grove Station, Burnley, as it looked around 1900. It was equipped with a telegraph office — and the once-familiar enamelled advertisements of the period.

Spring Vale Station, Darwen, about 1910. Opened in 1847, it was in fact a terminus on the Blackburn-Bolton line until the Sough Tunnel opened the following year. The station was called Sough until 1870 when it became Spring Vale and Sough and finally just Spring Vale in 1877. It closed in 1958. Prominent in the background is the massive chimney of India Mill.

Winter brought problems in the steam age if the water towers that filled the railway engines' tanks became frozen up. Here, at Blackburn Station in the 1950s, braziers are kept burning to keep the frost at bay.

Inside the booking office at Blackburn railway station in February 1952. The price of travel can be glimpsed on some of the ticket racks — the adult fare to London Euston, via Preston, cost 42s 9d and to Bolton, 2s 10d. Children travelled for exactly half-fare.

16 October 1929 — Eight of Blackburn Corporation's first buses are inspected outside the Town Hall. The council actually took delivery of 12 buses that month — six were 30-seat single-deck Leyland Tigers and six, 48-seat double-deck Leyland Titans, all of them petrol-engined. Their total cost was £18,315. Services commenced on six routes on 1 November. The last of the original buses was taken out of service in 1948.

1922 — this petrol-electric Tilling-Stevens bus, built in Maidstone, was the pride of the Rishton Motor Company's fleet. It provided a circular service between Rishton, Clayton-le-Moors, Great Harwood and Blackburn. The fare from Rishton to Blackburn was six old pence. The bus, equipped with solid tyres, had no clutch, gears or windscreen wiper. The petrol motor drove a dynamo which, in turn, provided drive to the back axle. The bus is pictured by the Load of Mischief pub at Clayton-le-Moors with its driver, Wallace Carnie, and conductor Wilfred Whittaker. The Rishton Motor Company merged with Antley Garage, near Church, in 1923 and later became part of Ribble Motors.

23 July 1908 — the scene at the end of a nightmare ride for members of Radcliffe and Whitefield Urban District Council. More than 25 of them had been on a tour of inspection of reservoirs at Scout Moor and Clough Bottom, being transported in a bus belonging to Rawtenstall Corporation. Passing over Crown Point, high above Burnley, one of the brakes on the bus failed, sending it on an ever-faster descent down the steep hill. One councillor leapt off soon into the terrorising trip, but the bus sped on, reaching up to 40mph. Near the Bull and Butcher pub, another six councillors abandoned ship. The vehicle careered on, hurtling down Cog Lane to the village of Gretna Green — where a cart loaded with stone setts stood in its path. Smashing into it, the bus severed the harness from the horse, but, amazingly, the animal escaped unharmed. Still unchecked, the bus — now also containing some of the cart's cargo — swerved up an embankment, ploughed through a hedge and came to rest in a field. The tally was more than 20 councillors severely shaken and three going home more seriously hurt, with injuries that included a broken leg, a fractured nose and serious cuts. Driver John Harker Maddocks escaped with a few scrapes.

Human error — someone forgot to switch the points as this locomotive, pulling a goods train, left Accrington in the early hours of 26 September 1899, bound for Hellifield — according to the schedule, that is. But, trapped on a siding line, it was heading for the buffers just above the gap between the twin bridges over Lonsdale Street. Its fireman leapt off as the crash approached, but the driver stayed at his post as the engine smashed through the obstruction, shattered the wall beyond and dived into the street below. So great was the impact that the engine's own buffers were sunk a foot deep into the road surface. But the fireman and driver, both from Wakefield, escaped unhurt.

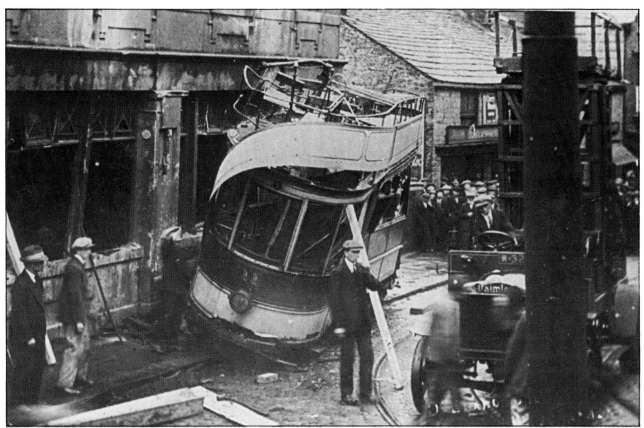

Fatal tram crash at Darwen — 20 September 1926. The No.11 Corporation tram was making the first journey of the day from Hoddlesden to Darwen when it ran out of control on the steep descent down Sudell Road, failed to take the sharp bend at the bottom of the hill and crashed into a billiard hall in Bridge Street. One man was killed and another died of his injuries the following day. Another seven were hurt, including the driver and conductor. One theory was that lightning may have affected the overhead trolley wire.

A Blackburn Corporation steam tram on Salford Bridge in the late 1890s, with buildings in New Water Street in the background. This tram served the Cemetery route, opened in 1888 by the London syndicate which brought trams to the town. It had a fleet of 14 steam engines and 16 passenger cars as well as 70 horses, with eight tramcars to pull. The crews worked a 14-hour day, six days a week and 12 hours on Sundays. But they got one day off in ten — when they were expected to give the tram a thorough cleaning. The Corporation acquired the tram undertaking in 1899 and began electrification that year. Steam trams were replaced on the Cemetery route in 1901 and the line extended to Wilpshire the following year. The last tram on the route ran on 21 December 1947.

2 August 1907 — thousands lined the route from Accrington to Oswaldtwistle for the introduction of electric tram cars on the line serving the two towns. It was an event that spelled the end of Accrington's 'Baltic Fleet' of steam-hauled trams which had begun running in 1886. The new trams running up Union Road to Oswaldtwistle were all single-deck — because the railway bridge over the road near Church station was too low for double-deck trams to pass under. Here, the Mayoress of Accrington, accompanied by her husband, Councillor T.G.Higham drives the inaugural tram car. By the last full year of electric tram operation — up to April 1928 — Accrington's trams had covered almost 14.3 million miles and carried nearly 169 million passengers — without a single death or serious injury. Accrington's last tram ran on 6 January 1932, on the Burnley Road section. Five of Accrington's trams, however, carried on running elsewhere — Sunderland and Llandudno each buying two and Lytham St Anne's taking another.

This tram was one of five which took part in the official inauguration of the first electric trams on the Accrington-Oswaldtwistle line in August 1907. Only the first and last trams in the procession were decorated with flags. Civic dignitaries filled four of the tramcars, but this looks like the one which members of the public were allowed to board on the big occasion. The lady at the tiller (right) is either former Accrington Mayoress, Mrs Rawson, or Mrs A.S.Bury, both of whom drove trams in the official parade — thanks to their husbands' positions as aldermen. Note the working-class fashions — cloth caps, clogs, Eton collars and knee-breeches for the boys; shawls for the lasses.

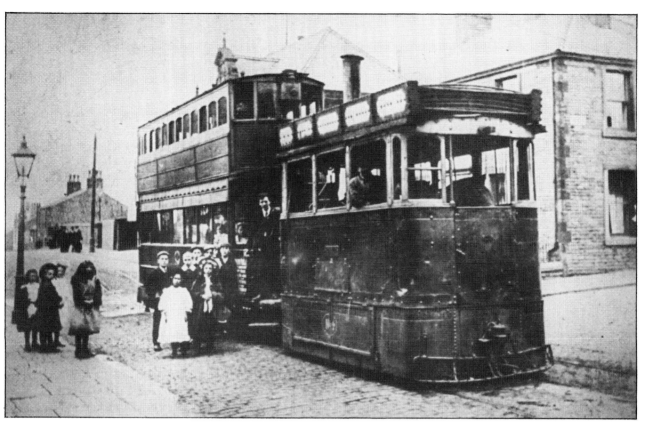

A 'farewell' souvenir postcard picture of one of Accrington's last steam trams, taken in 1907 on Whalley Road, Clayton-le-Moors. "Though lost to sight, To Memory Dear," said the original caption.

A Blackburn Corporation tram at the Billinge terminus on Preston New Road, with Revidege Road at the right. Tram No.33 was one of eight built in 1898 by G.F.Milnes & Company, of Birkenhead, using Siemens electrical equipment. The driver, like the upper-deck passengers, was exposed to all weathers. But soon after World War One, canopies were built over the platforms and glass screens fitted. From their introduction in 1899 until 1905, the Corporation lost £34,000 running electric tram services, but afterwards they became a big money-earner. Blackburn's trams were painted olive green and ivory. Note the postman wearing an old-style shako helmet in the group at the right.

A single-deck tramcar climbs Manchester Road, Burnley, past the Rose and Crown Hotel. The town began the switch to electric trams in 1901 after introducing steam trams in 1881. Burnley's first steamer broke down in Westgate on its trial run and had to be hauled back to the depot by a horse. The next one exploded on its first outing. And several prosecutions for smoke emission from the tramways' steam locos resulted in them temporarily being withdrawn in favour of horse-drawn trams. Burnley's last tram ran in 1935, three years after the first bus services were established.

Blackburn's last tram left the Boulevard for the Intack depot shortly after 11.30pm on 3 September 1949. Specially illuminated for the occasion, it was driven by Transport Committee chairman, Councillor Robert Weir, with the Mayor and Mayoress and council members and officials as passengers. At Intack, Councillor Weir was besieged by autograph hunters and, along the route, many people placed pennies on the tramlines — to be crushed as souvenirs. But at the depot, Mr Arthur Potts took over the helm for the honour of driving the last tram into the shed, having done the same with the town's last steam tram nearly 50 years before.

War and Weather

1916 — Six-year-old Jennie Jackson takes the salute at Burnley Town Hall. Kitted out as 'Young Kitchener' — after Britain's World War One military supremo — she played a big part in a drive launched by her mother to provide comforts for the troops. The effort raised more than £4,000.

February 1915 — the Mayor of Accrington, Councillor John Harwood, with officers of the 11th Battalion of the East Lancashire Regiment — the ill-fated Accrington Pals. They and their men — volunteers for Kitchener's 'New Army' raised the year before — were decimated in the first day of the Battle of the Somme on 1 July 1916. Of the 700 Pals who advanced to the German lines that morning, 235 were killed and 350 were wounded in less than 20 minutes by German machine-guns and artillery that was supposed to have been obliterated by a seven-day barrage by British artillery.

31 August 1940 — the second bombing raid in Blackburn and the second within 24 hours. Just before midnight, a single bomb struck Ainsworth Street in the town centre where the day's last trams and buses were being drawn up. The driver of one tram died from shock and his conductor died later from his injuries. The bomb wrecked two shops and smashed the fronts of several others. Three trams and four buses were also damaged. The previous day, a bomb hit a house in Bennington Street, but the occupants were unhurt.

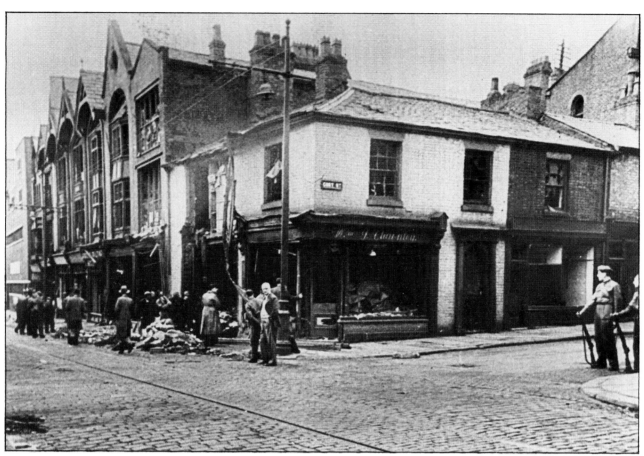

Seen from another angle, the aftermath of the August 1940 air-raid on Ainsworth Street, Blackburn. Tailor Mr William J.Charnley, owner of the shop on the corner with Cort Street, left a notice in the wrecked premises telling customers that the business had been 'Blown Around The Corner'. One theory was that the German bomber pilot had seen the electric flashes of the overhead tram wires, had mistaken them for gunfire and dropped a bomb in reply.

World War Two Home Guard soldiers training in bomb disposal — with dummy explosives — by the railway at Church. The date is uncertain, but with the Home Guard — originally the Local Defence Volunteers — being raised in May 1940, when invasion fears were at their peak, and the Nazi air-raids largely petering out by early 1942, this picture was probably taken in the interim.

19 October 1940. This was the devastation in Darwen after four bombs fell — on Alice Street, Police Street and near Hollins Paper Mill and close to Woodfold Mill. Several houses were damaged, including this one in Stansfield Street. There were several casualties, but only one needing hospital treatment. Note the anti-blast tape on the windows in the background.

Back with a vengeance. Just two days after Darwen's first air-raid, the Luftwaffe returned. On 21 October 1940, a sneak daylight raider dropped three bombs in a town-centre back street, flattening houses in Crown Street and Holme Street. The plane also machine-gunned a Corporation bus as it sped away. Six people were killed instantly and a seventh died from injuries five months later. Here firemen and workmen are seen in a bomb crater in Crown Street.

The Ribble Valley village of Chatburn was the target for two German bombs on 30 October 1940. The raid took place in broad daylight. One bomb completely demolished a house and the other exploded on the roadway, making the post office and several houses uninhabitable. A petrol lorry was hurled into the driveway of a house and blazing fuel ran down the highway. The tanker driver and two other people were killed. Five others were detained in hospital and many more treated for minor injuries. Here, the wrecked vehicle lies amid the ruins in the village centre. Altogether, 16 people were killed in East Lancashire in the 1940-41 blitz.

Blackburn, Spring 1943, No.1 Mobile Company of the Home Guard marches past the General Post Office in Darwen Street during a 'Wings for Victory' campaign.

Fog on Blackburn Boulevard in 1965. Anti-pollution and clean-air legislation have helped to make 'pea soup' conditions like these mostly a memory.

January 1940 — after the white-out winter that paralysed East Lancashire. This picture was taken at the top of Manchester Road, Burnley, where digging parties, helped by troops, took a whole week to get to vehicles stranded there. Traffic was also brought to a standstill in towns across the region. It was six days after the blizzard stopped before trains were able to reach Blackburn and mills were shut down for a week.

Revidge Road, Blackburn, in 1947 — one of the four coldest winters of the century in East Lancashire. That year severe weather lasted until the middle of March and conditions were made worse by a chronic fuel shortage.

The curse of the 1963 winter was frozen water pipes. Hundreds of householders like these in Parsonage Road, Blackburn, were forced to rely on standpipes for weeks. Down the road at the frozen-up Rising Sun Inn on Whalley New Road, the brewery delivered water supplies by barrel along with the beer. With the thaw, came the widespread nightmare of burst pipes.

The Shooters' Arms in Southfield Lane, Nelson, was swamped by snow in the Big Freeze of 1963. The seemingly-endless winter of snow and ice began to do its worst on Boxing Day the previous year and there was no thaw until the weather finally turned mild at the beginning of March.

Subscribers

Presentation Copies

Councillor Paul Browne, Mayor of Blackburn and Darwen
Councillor John Greenwood, Mayor of Burnley
Councillor Sonia Bramley-Haworth, Mayor of Accrington
Councillor Roy Clarkson, Mayor of Pendle
Councillor Tony Jackson, Mayor of Ribble Valley

1 Peter Tattersall
2 J Clarke
3 Mr Brian Horsfield
4 John James Dixon
5 Frank Ashworth
6 John Lambert
7 David Hunt
8 Val Watkinson
9 Frank Bartram
10 Sheila Mary Baybutt
11 Cyril & Rita Holden
12 Norman Forrest
13 John Westwell
14 Eric Gibbons
15 Jim Haworth
16 Mr M O'Hara
17 Mr J Holden
18 E Holden
19 Harold Gibson
20 Mr & Mrs Roy Y Ashworth
21 Jack Westwell
22 Stephen Livesey
23 Mr G E Hurlbut
24 Michael Picton
25 Margaret Hilton
26 Gordon Hartley
27 J & M Beardsworth
28 R Hawthornthwaite
29 William Davidson
30 W Davies
31 Frank Coyne
32 Mr & Mrs S B Houldsworth
33 Brian Rushton
34 G C Haworth
35 R B Smith
36 David J Boultwood
37 Sheila Allen
38 William Boyes
39 Colin V Redmayne
40 Meryl Veitch
41 Mr John Taylor
42 Norma Cox
43 Leslie Whittaker
44 Keith F Blackshaw
45 T C Sebastian
46 William Binns
47 Marlene Talbot
48 Peter R J Davies
49 Mr & Mrs R Walsh
50 Clifford Cross